5

IN DEFENCE OF SHELLEY

&

OTHER ESSAYS

BY

HERBERT READ

Essay Index Reprint Series

BOOKS FOR LIBRARIES PRESS
FREEPORT, NEW YORK

First Published 1936
Reprinted 1968

LIBRARY OF CONGRESS CATALOG CARD NUMBER:
68-26470

PRINTED IN THE UNITED STATES OF AMERICA

NOTE

THE leading essay in this volume, "In Defence of Shelley," is here published for the first time. The others have either wholly or in part appeared separately: "Coventry Patmore" in a volume of essays by various hands entitled *Great Victorians* (Ivor Nicholson & Watson, *n.d.*) and "Pablo Picasso" in a similar volume entitled *Great Contemporaries* (Cassell & Co., 1934). "Gerard Manley Hopkins" was first printed in *English Critical Essays Twentieth Century* (Oxford University Press, 1933). The two notes on Swift, and the essay on "Diderot's Love Letters" are reprinted with some revision from *The Times Literary Supplement*. "Obscurity in English Poetry" has been so much rewritten that its previous history is of no account. "Parallels in English Painting and Poetry" was originally delivered as a public lecture at the University of London, and "English Art" is reprinted from *The Burlington Magazine*.

H.R.

November, 1935.

CONTENTS

IN DEFENCE OF SHELLEY

I

THE first collected edition of Shelley's poems was published in 1839. His reputation was then already considerable, but it steadily rose for fifty years, reaching a kind of zenith with the publication of Dowden's *Life* in 1886. Dowden had been immediately preceded by W. M. Rossetti, J. A. Symonds, J. C. Jeaffreson and William Sharp, and practically the whole of that literary generation was given over to an uncritical hero-worship of the poet, which inevitably led to a reaction. Now, another fifty years on, we are at the bottom of the trough—at a depth plumbed by Mr. Eliot on February 17th, 1933, in a lecture delivered at Harvard University.* The romantic optimism of Professor Dowden is neatly balanced by the romantic pessimism of Professor Eliot, but a true critical judgment is satisfied with neither extreme. A judgment without prejudice is likely to arrive at some intermediate position, but since for the moment the verdict has gone against the poet, I call this attempt at redress a defence of Shelley.

Shelley has always had his enemies. For the most part they have been what we might call political enemies. Caring little for literature as such, these critics of the poet have fastened on his social and

The Use of Poetry and the Use of Criticism. By T. S. Eliot, pp.87–102.

ethical ideas and have seen in them a subversive influence to be opposed with all the powers of law and tradition. With such critics we are not really concerned; they no longer count in the controversy, for Shelley has been universally acknowledged as a poet, and his poetry is part of our culture. To dethrone Shelley it is no longer sufficient to prove his atheism or his communism, or any other form of intellectual perversion; the critic must destroy his reputation as a poet, trusting that then he will silently disappear from our Parnassus carrying with him his dangerous load of mischief.

A frontal attack on the poetry would not be very effective. You may say that this poem or that poem is bad, but however many reasons you bring forward to support your opinion, an opinion and a personal opinion it remains. Your audience will simply register their disagreement, and continue to admire the poetry in their own way. But if somehow you can imply that it is rather bad form to admire Shelley's poetry, that it is the mark of an inferior taste, of muddled thought and vulgar sensibility, then you will set up a sort of fashionable inhibition far more powerful in its effect and far wider in its range. People will not like Shelley's poetry because they will not read it. His reputation will die of neglect.

The first necessity, therefore, will be a position of moral and intellectual superiority; a consequent air of condescension. Coleridge first suggested these tactics, but with the safeguard of his infinite humility and understanding:

4

"I think as highly of Shelley's genius—yea, and of his *heart*—as you can do. Soon after he left Oxford, he went to the lakes, poor fellow! and with some wish, I have understood, to see me; but I was absent, and Southey received him instead. Now— the very reverse of what would have been the case in ninety-nine instances of a hundred—I *might* have been of use to him, and Southey could not; for I should have sympathised with his poetics, meta-physical reveries, and the very word metaphysics is an abomination to Southey, and Shelley would have felt that I understood him. His discussions— tending towards atheism of a certain sort—would not have scared *me*; for *me* it would have been a semi-transparent larva, soon to be sloughed, and through which I should have seen the true *image*— the final metamorphosis. Besides, I have ever thought that sort of atheism the next best religion to Christianity; nor does the better faith I have learnt from Paul and John interfere with the cordial reverence I feel for Benedict Spinoza."*

There is a generosity about Coleridge's sympathy which is very disarming; but there is also a fatal quality of pity. There is an assumption that Shelley was weak, or stumbling, or even blind, and that he,

*This is quoted from a letter of Coleridge's by Hogg (*Life*, ch. xiv). The same gist is given in a conversation with Coleridge recorded by J. H. Frere (see the Nonesuch *Coleridge*, p. 481). "Shelley was a man of great power as a poet, and could he only have had some plane whereon to stand, and look down upon his own mind, he would have succeeded. There are flashes of the true spirit to be met with in his works. Poor Shelley, it is a pity I often think that I never met with him. I could have done him good. . . ." etc.

Coleridge, could be *of some use* to him. But this, as we shall see, is an entirely gratuitous assumption. Such as were Shelley's opinions at this time (in 1815) they were opinions honestly arrived at, and held by the poet with no essential variations to the day of his death.

It is difficult to find any excuses for the insufferable superiority of Matthew Arnold. His essay on Shelley, a review of Dowden's *Life*, is even from a literary point of view about as poor a piece of work as Arnold ever perpetrated. Its very style is infected with prejudice and disdain. In matter it is little more than a summary of Dowden's volumes, ending with that sublime sneer: What a set! Arnold, we are made to feel, had formed an ideal image of Shelley, a Shelley suggested by Hogg's description of the poet which Arnold had written down the first time he read it, and had always borne in his mind: "Nor was the moral expression less beautiful than the intellectual; for there was a softness, a delicacy, a gentleness, and especially (though this may surprise many) that air of profound religious veneration that characterises the best works and chiefly the frescoes (and into these they infused their whole souls) of the great masters of Florence and of Rome." Dowden, in his blind and blundering way, had shattered this image—had forced upon us "much in him which is ridiculous and odious." The image, Arnold tried to persuade himself, still subsisted; but "with many a scar and stain; never again will it have the same pureness and beauty which it had formerly." In the bitterness of his disillusion Arnold resorts to strong words—words whose force is not mitigated by their foreignness. "It is a sore trial for our love of Shelley. What a set! what a world! is the exclamation that breaks from us as we come to an end of this history of 'the occurrences of Shelley's private life,' I used the French word *bête* for a letter of Shelley's; for the world in which we find him I can only use another French word, *sale*."

Such righteous indignation sounds merely comical to-day, but we have no reason to doubt its sincerity. To recover the background of moral snobbery from which it proceeded would need a considerable effort of imagination; and it would be an effort wasted. Arnold, to do him justice, did not let his moral prejudice altogether obliterate his literary judgment. In the essay from which I have quoted, he excuses himself dealing with Shelley's poetry for want of space—warning us, however, that the poetry would not get off unscathed. "Let no one suppose that a want of humour and a self-delusion such as Shelley's have no effect upon a man's poetry. The man Shelley, in very truth, is not entirely sane, and Shelley's poetry is not entirely sane either." And then he ends by repeating, from his essay on Byron, that trumpery phrase of which he was evidently so proud, about the beautiful and ineffectual angel "beating in the void his luminous wings in vain."

I have said that we find Arnold's attitude comical to-day; but perhaps I should have said that we find the expression he gave to his attitude comical. For if

7

we were all agreed that the whole pother raised by Arnold could now be dismissed as one of the minor absurdities of the Victorian age, there would be no need for this essay in defence of Shelley. But Arnold's attitude has been repeated in our time by no less a critic than Mr. T. S. Eliot, in the lecture already mentioned. But in Mr. Eliot's case we shall find that the overt emphasis is not so much on the poet's morals, as on his ideas. Naturally the ideas cannot be separated from the morals, nor either from the poetry; but, before a modern audience, a master of critical strategy could not fail to concentrate his attack on the ideas.

Mr. Eliot's main charge against Shelley is one of intellectual incoherence. Incidentally he reveals a pretty strong distaste for the poet's personality, which is perhaps a logical consequence of the main charge. At the risk of some distortion I must give a summary of the whole indictment. "The ideas of Shelley," Mr. Eliot begins, "seem to me always to be ideas of adolescence. . . . And an enthusiasm for Shelley seems to me also to be an affair of adolescence. . . . I find his ideas repellent; and the difficulty of separating Shelley from his ideas and beliefs is still greater than with Wordsworth. And the biographical interest which Shelley has always excited makes it difficult to read the poetry without remembering the man: and the man was humourless, pedantic, self-centred, and sometimes almost a blackguard. Except for an occasional flash of shrewd sense, when he is speaking of someone else and not concerned with his own affairs or with fine writing, his letters are insufferably dull." So far the items in the charge are almost the same as Arnold's, only a little more restrained in formulation. But after a page or so of concessions, Mr. Eliot returns to his main point: "But some of Shelley's views I positively dislike, and that hampers my enjoyment of the poems in which they occur; and others seem to me so puerile that I cannot enjoy the poems in which they occur." This leads to a discussion of the now famous problem of Belief and Poetry, and to the conclusion, in respect of Shelley, that "when the doctrine, theory, belief or 'view of life' presented in a poem is one which the mind of the reader can accept as coherent, mature, and founded on the facts of experience, it interposes no obstacle to the reader's enjoyment, whether it be one that he accept or deny, approve or deprecate. When it is one which the reader rejects as childish or feeble, it may, for a reader of well-developed mind, set up an almost complete check. . . . I can only regret that Shelley did not live to put his poetic gifts, which were certainly of the first order, at the service of more tenable beliefs—which need not have been, for my purposes, beliefs more acceptable to me."

I propose, by way of answering this general charge against Shelley, to establish two points; the maturity and permanent worth of his best poetry, and the irrelevance of that mare's-nest of Belief, first introduced into the discussion of poetry by our tortuous logodædalist, Dr. I. A. Richards. Incidentally I shall

9

suggest that Shelley's ideas do not deserve the scorn heaped upon them by Mr. Eliot, whose attitude, in common with Coleridge's and Arnold's, is based on simpler if obscurer psychological reactions. In these reactions more poets and greater poets than Shelley are involved—Goethe, for example, of whom Mr. Eliot writes: "it is perhaps truer to say that he dabbled in both philosophy and poetry and made no great success of either." It will be found, I fancy, that it is not really poetry that is involved—not the actual recognition or definition of poetry in specific instances. When beliefs do not enter into the question—as in the case of Landor or of Keats—then I think Mr. Eliot and I would find a complete measure of agreement. But for some reason Mr. Eliot's taste in poetry is not so catholic as mine—it does not embrace Shelley and Goethe, for example. Mr. Eliot attempts to justify his exclusiveness on critical grounds; he only succeeds in betraying an irrational prejudice. In the process he bears false witness, not so much against poetry itself, as against the nature of the poet.

II

Obviously my first concern must be to vindicate the high value of Shelley's poetry. It is curious that all these detractors of the poetry make vague but generous gestures of acceptance which are at variance with their detailed statements. To Coleridge Shelley is "a man of great power as a poet"; Arnold speaks of "the charm of the man's writings—of Shelley's poetry. It is his poetry, above everything else, which for many people establishes that he is an angel." As for Mr. Eliot, though he confesses that he never opens the volume of his poems "simply because I want to read poetry, but only with some special reason for reference," yet, as we have seen, Shelley's poetic gifts "were certainly of the first order." Not a critical judgment, but some moral asceticism, would seem to be the basis of Mr. Eliot's disdain. He does, it is true, accuse Shelley of "a good deal which is just bad jingling," but he admits that *The Triumph of Life* is a great though unfinished poem. He admits to liking the last stanza of *Prometheus Unbound*. But this is about as far as his direct statements about the poetry go; for the rest, he is "thoroughly gravelled," not by the poems themselves, but by the "shabby" ideas expressed in them.

At first Shelley's own attitude towards poetry as an art, and towards his own poetry in particular, seems to be decidedly treacherous. As early as 1813, when engaged on his first considerable poem, *Queen Mab*, we find him taking up an attitude which implies a certain contempt for the formal aspects of poetry. At the same time, from the very beginning, what we might in our modern fashion call an indifference to pure poetry is combined with what we would least expect—an avoidance of didactic poetry. Writing to Hogg in the year mentioned, Shelley says: "My poems will, I fear, little stand the criticism even of friendship; some of the latter ones have the merit of conveying a meaning in every word, and all are faithful pictures of my feelings at the time of writing them. But they are, in a great measure, abrupt and obscure—all breathing hatred of despotism and bigotry; but, I think, not too openly for publication. One fault they are indisputably exempt from, that of being a volume of fashionable literature." This would seem to be a fair confession of didacticism, but a few weeks later, writing to the same correspondent, he makes a much more positive statement to the contrary effect: "*Queen Mab* will be in ten cantos, and will contain about twenty-eight hundred lines; the other poems contain probably as much more. The notes to *Queen Mab* will be long and philosophical; I shall take that opportunity, which I judge to be a safe one, of submitting for public discussion principles of reformation, which I decline to do syllogistically in the poem. A poem very didactic is, I think, very stupid." This distinction between poetry which is philosophical and yet at the same time not didactic deserves more examination than it has been given by critics of Shelley; it is important for our conception of Shelley's life and personality, as well as for any exact judgment on his poetry. Considering the strength of Shelley's moral and political views, it is a great proof of his instinctive sense of the limits of the art that he never for a moment thought of using poetry as an instrument of propaganda. Even as late as 1819 he could write (in a letter to Peacock): "I consider

12

poetry very subordinate to moral and political science, and if I were well, certainly I would aspire to the latter, for I can conceive a great work, embodying the discoveries of all ages, and harmonizing the contending creeds by which mankind have been ruled." And this, in spite of the intervening *Defence of Poetry* in which he deepened and yet clarified his philosophy, remained his feeling to the end; for in his last letter to Peacock, written in the year of his death, he confesses: "I wish I had something better to do than furnish this jingling food for the hunger of oblivion, called verse, but I have not; and since you give me no encouragement about India I cannot hope to have." In a footnote Peacock informs us that Shelley had expressed a desire to be employed politically at the court of a native prince.

The poet, especially an original poet like Shelley, is always conscious of the limited effect of all his work. "*Prometheus* was never intended for more than five or six persons," he wrote in a letter to Gisborne, and for a poet with "a passion for reforming the world" this is a bitter realisation. It would be an intolerable realisation were there no compensations in prospect; and what is in prospect is a matter of faith—of faith in one's appeal to a jury "impanelled by Time from the selectest of the wise of many generations." It will be noticed that this jury is of the wise, and not merely of the sensitive; and Shelley uses the word deliberately. For whilst avoiding like the plague the didactic use of poetry, Shelley is far from that theory of pure poetry, which would exempt poetry from any useful effect whatsoever. Poetry might after all be an essential process in the great work of regenerating mankind—a preparation of the mind for the seeds of moral and political science, which otherwise might fall on rocky ground. The image is not a very noble one, but there are one or two statements of Shelley's which will give it a full idealistic force: for example, this from the Preface to *Prometheus Unbound*: "For my part I had rather be damned with Plato and Lord Bacon, than go to Heaven with Paley and Malthus. But it is a mistake to suppose that I dedicate my poetical compositions solely to the direct enforcement of reform, or that I consider them in any degree as containing a reasoned system on the theory of human life. Didactic poetry is my abhorrence; nothing can be equally well expressed in prose that is not tedious and supererogatory in verse. My purpose has hitherto been simply to familiarise the highly refined imagination of the more select classes of poetical readers with beautiful idealisms of moral excellence; aware that until the mind can love, and admire, and trust, and hope, and endure, reasoned principles of moral conduct are seeds cast upon the highway of life which the unconscious passenger tramples into dust, although they would bear the harvest of his happiness."

In a cancelled passage from the Preface to *Adonais* Shelley introduces the notion of "sympathy," which we may find useful: "If I understand myself, I have written neither for profit nor for fame. I have employed my poetical compositions and publications simply as the instruments of that sympathy between myself and others which the ardent and unbounded love I cherished for my kind incited me to acquire." But the most explicit statement of his aims comes in the *Defence of Poetry*, there given a generalisation and philosophical dignity which make that essay the profoundest treatment of the subject in the English language. The essay opens with a distinction between reason and imagination which is the fundamental distinction for the whole of this question, and which is a proof, if any were required, of the precision with which Shelley used his terms. The two modes of mental action are distinguished as "mind contemplating the relations borne by one thought to another, however produced," and as "mind acting upon those thoughts so as to colour them with its own light, and composing from them, as from elements, other thoughts, each containing within itself the principle of its own integrity." Reason is analysis, or "the enumeration of quantities already known"; imagination is synthesis, or "the perception of the value of those quantities, both separately and as a whole. Reason respects the differences, and imagination the similitudes of things. Reason is to the imagination as the instrument to the agent . . ."

Poetry is then defined as the instrument of the imagination, as distinct from science, which is the instrument of the reason. But poetry acts in a way peculiar to itself; "it awakens and enlarges the mind itself by rendering it the receptacle of a thousand unapprehended combinations of thought." These combinations of thought are due to that principle of sympathy already referred to, which is not only the mode of action typical of poetry, but also of morals. This identification of poetry and morality must be dealt with separately, but for the moment we will keep to the poetic process, which is further defined as an enlargement of the circumference of the imagination "by replenishing it with thoughts of every new delight, which have the power of attracting and assimilating to their own nature all other thoughts, and which form new intervals and interstices whose void forever craves fresh food. Poetry strengthens the faculty which is the organ of the moral nature of man, in the same manner as exercise strengthens a limb."

This dynamical, this almost physical conception of poetry, is extended in other directions which show how closely Shelley observed the psychological nature of his own activity. The ranging, gathering, accumulative character of the poetic process is not its only function; the materials poetry attracts to itself must be controlled, and a desire is therefore engendered in the mind to reproduce and arrange these materials "according to a certain rhythm and order which may be called the beautiful and the good." But such rhythm and order can only be engendered in the unconscious mind. "Poetry is not like reasoning, a power to be exerted according to the determination of the will. A man cannot say,

'I will compose poetry.' The greatest poet even cannot say it; for the mind in creation is as a fading coal, which some invisible influence, like an inconstant wind, awakens to transitory brightness; this power arises from within, like the colour of a flower which fades and changes as it is developed, and the conscious portions of our natures are unprophetic either of its approach or its departure." Nevertheless, and this is an observation which a less scrupulous psychologist might have omitted, "the frequent recurrence of the poetical power . . . may produce in the mind a habit of order and harmony correlative with its own nature and with its effects upon other minds."

The *Defence of Poetry* is an uncompleted essay, and it would be unreasonable to complain that it leaves many problems of poetry undiscussed. We miss, in particular, Shelley's observations on the technique of poetry. In a sense he was singularly uninterested in the subject, being content to take over the prevailing diction, which was, indeed, the reformed diction of Coleridge and Wordsworth. But there is little evidence that he had their reforming zeal, and if it suited his purpose he was just as ready to take over the technique of Spenser or Milton. He refers to *Adonais* as "a highly-wrought *piece of art*," which is curiously suggestive of the attitude against which Wordsworth had revolted. On the other hand, in the *Defence of Poetry* he admits innovation as a necessary principle in verse. "An observation of the regular mode of the recurrence of harmony in the language of poetical minds, together with its relation to music, produced metre, or a certain system of traditional forms of harmony and language. Yet it is by no means essential that a poet should accommodate his language to this traditional form, so that harmony, which is its spirit, be observed. The practice is indeed convenient and popular, and to be preferred, especially in such composition as includes much action: but every great poet must inevitably innovate upon the example of his predecessors in the exact structure of his peculiar versification." And what he meant by this last phrase he had explained on a previous page, in a passage which shows how innately sound his poetic practice was—being based, as all true poetry must be based, on the material qualities of language. "Language, colour, form, and religious and civil habits of action, are all the instruments and materials of poetry. . . . But poetry in a more restricted sense expresses those arrangements of language, and especially metrical language, which are created by that imperial faculty, whose throne is curtained within the invisible nature of man. And this springs from the nature itself of language, which is a more direct representation of the actions and passions of our internal being, and is susceptible of more various and delicate combinations, than colour, form, or motion, and is more plastic and obedient to the control of that faculty of which it is the creation. For language is arbitrarily produced by the imagination, and has relation to thoughts alone; but all other materials, instruments, and conditions of art, have relations among each other, which limit and interpose between conception and expression." He then contrasts poetry, in this respect, with the arts of sculpture, painting, and music, and concludes that such arts can never equal poetry as an expression of the immediacy of thought.

Such a clear perception of the nature of poetry does not necessarily imply an ability to put precept into practice, and since the precepts were a late product of his short life, we must be prepared for much immature prentice work. For Shelley began publishing whilst still a boy at school, and in spite of his hero Godwin's opinion that early authorship was detrimental to the cause of general happiness, during the rest of his life his productions were sent to the press with almost indecent haste. Shelley always had the itch to see himself in print, and as heir to a fortune, if not in actual possession of money, he could always find a ready publisher. His collected poems, in the standard Oxford edition, make a volume of a thousand pages. How much of this bulk Shelley himself would have suppressed it would be presumptuous to guess; but any true friend of Shelley would willingly unload half of it into oblivion, and even some proportion of the rest he would only keep, as Mr. Eliot keeps the lot, for reference. A decisive change came in the year 1816, a year in which Shelley wrote very little, in which his poetic faculty seemed to lie fallow, numbed by domestic anxieties— the hostility of the Westbrooks, the intransigence of Godwin, ill-health, the lack of money. At the end of that year came Harriet's suicide, from which he sought some relief in the concentration of composition—the result being *The Revolt of Islam*, a poem of 4,818 lines. There was concentration only in the act, not in the issue. To follow Shelley's poetic development is like following the course of a mighty river, from mouth to source: at first everything is wide, even and aqueous, but as we proceed the stream narrows and the surface breaks, flowing with a more obvious force and music—an image perhaps suggested by the subject-matter of *The Revolt of Islam*. Shelley tells us in his Preface that his object was "to enlist the harmony of metrical language, the ethereal combinations of the fancy, the rapid and subtle transitions of human passion, all those elements which essentially compose a Poem, in the cause of a liberal and comprehensive morality. . . . For this purpose I have chosen a story of human passion in its most universal character, diversified with moving and romantic adventures, and appealing, in contempt of all artificial opinions or institutions, to the common sympathies of every human breast. . . . The Poem therefore . . . is narrative, not didactic. It is a succession of pictures illustrating the growth and progress of individual mind aspiring after excellence, and devoted to the love of mankind . . ." The very phrases—a succession of pictures, ethereal combinations of the fancy—do not promise a coherent form; and when Shelley further informs the reader that he has chosen the Spenserian stanza because he was enticed "by the brilliancy and magnificence of sound which a mind that has been nourished upon musical thoughts can produce by a just and harmonious arrangement of the pauses of this measure," that reader should not be surprised to find a poem whose action is dissipated in incident, whose theme is lost in a jungle of imagery. We seem to drift aimlessly always in some kind of boat or bark, upon some torrent or flood; and it is only in the last line of the poem that we find a haven, uncertain of the way we have come, indifferent, after so much wandering, to our destiny:

> Motionless resting on the lake awhile,
> > I saw its marge of snow-bright mountains rear
> Their peaks aloft, I saw each radiant isle,
> > And in the midst, afar, even like a sphere
> > Hung in one hollow sky, did there appear
> The Temple of the Spirit; on the sound
> > Which issued thence, drawn nearer and more near,
> Like the swift moon this glorious earth around,
> The charmèd boat approached, and there its haven found.

This last stanza is representative enough of all the five hundred odd which compose the poem; Shelley uses his measure with mastery, and where he fails, in comparison with Spenser, is not in the mere manipulation of words, but in their choice. Spenser was very particular about his words; even pedantic. Shelley confesses, in his Preface, to an indifference on this very point: "Nor have I permitted any system relating to mere words to divert the attention of the reader, from whatever interest I may have succeeded in creating, to my own ingenuity in contriving to disgust them according to the rules of criticism. I have simply clothed my thoughts in what appeared to me the most obvious and appropriate language. A person familiar with nature, and with the most celebrated productions of the human mind, can scarcely err in following the instinct, with respect to selection of language, produced by that familiarity." There is obviously some oblique reference here— perhaps to Wordsworth's Preface to his Poems published in 1815. But though Shelley is right, in so far as he is relying on the subconscious origination of appropriate language (according to the theory he was, as we have seen, to state explicitly in *A Defence of Poetry*), yet there is in this passage a certain un- easiness, a certain anticipation of criticism, which is a confession of self-criticism. In a letter replying to Godwin's criticism of the poem, Shelley says: "The poem was produced by a series of thoughts which filled my mind with unbounded and sustained enthusiasm. I felt the precariousness of my life, and I engaged in this task, resolved to leave some record of myself. Much of what the volume contains was written with the same feeling—as real, though not so prophetic—as the communications of a dying man." Shelley, we might say, always wrote with one eye on posterity and the other on his tomb; and the feverish haste entailed by such an attitude leads to qualities which the most sympathetic critic cannot excuse. There is not a single long composition of Shelley which does not suffer from prolixity, from lack of those most precious qualities of precision and objectivity. At the same time we must not blame Shelley for failing to express qualities which were not in his nature; certain human features and faculties are antithetical, and we are asking for a monster if we look for them all in the same personality. Shelley, as we shall see later, was not a "visuel"; he was a transcendentalist, for whom words are never sufficient for the vision they must express.

This question, the fundamental one for the appreciation of Shelley's poetry, had better be discussed in relation to a more considerable poem than *The Revolt of Islam*. If I dismiss *The Revolt of Islam*, it is not because I think it can be ignored; it is a poem of many individual beauties, and even if the whole is "sick with excess of sweetness," there is throughout a spirit of intellectual energy which lifts it into significance, making it a part, if only a prelude, of Shelley's great achievement. That achievement, in its strictly poetic aspects, is represented by *Prometheus Unbound*, written little more than a year after *The Revolt of Islam*, by *Epipsychidion* and *Adonais*, written the year before his death, and by various shorter odes and lyrics, all written in the last four years of his life. These three groups have certain characteristics in common, and possibly they merge into one another; but they have qualities which are distinct enough to justify a separate classification.

In concentrating on these three groups we shall be neglecting certain works of which perhaps *The Cenci* is the only one which must be explained away—other notable poems, such as *The Witch of Atlas*, *Hellas*, and *The Triumph of Life*, I regard as conforming in every way to the characteristics of one or other of the typical poems mentioned. But *The Cenci* is a different matter. Byron called it "sad work," and if not for the same reason ("the subject renders it so") I agree with this judgment of a friend and contemporary of the poet. For Shelley it was an experiment—an attempt to be objective, *sachlich*. But he was writing against the grain of his personality, and knew it. "Those writings which I have hitherto published," he tells Leigh Hunt in a Dedicatory Letter, "have been little else than visions which impersonate my own apprehensions of the beautiful and the just. I can also perceive in them the literary defects incidental to youth and impatience; they are dreams of what ought to be, or may be. The drama which I now present to you is a sad reality. I lay aside the presumptuous attitude of an instructor, and am content to paint, with such colours as my own heart furnishes, that which has been." It was a brave gesture, but doomed to failure. Far from the subject being the cause of this failure, it is its very horror which compels a certain dramatic vitality, and makes it even possible to act the drama with some effect. But as poetry, both in the limited sense as blank verse and in the general sense as the creation of poetic character and atmosphere, it does not begin to be a great tragedy. It is a pastiche of Elizabethan drama, of Webster in particular, and as a form has no originality and lacks that "something wholly new and

24

relative to the age" which Shelley recognised in *Don Juan* and longed to possess. Even at its most forceful the verse is wooden, unnatural.

> *How comes this hair undone?*
> *Its wandering strings must be what blind me so,*
> *And yet I tied it fast.—O, horrible!*
> *The pavement sinks under my feet! The walls*
> *Spin round! I see a woman weeping there,*
> *And standing calm and motionless, whilst I*
> *Slide giddily as the world reels. . . . My God!*
> *The beautiful blue heaven is flecked with blood!*
> *The sunshine on the floor is black! The air*
> *Is changed to vapours such as the dead breathe*
> *In charnel pits! Pah! I am choked! There creeps*
> *A clinging, black contaminating mist*
> *About me . . . 'tis substantial, heavy, thick,*
> *I cannot pluck it from me, for it glues*
> *My fingers and my limbs to one another,*
> *And eats into my sinews, and dissolves*
> *My flesh to a pollution, poisoning*
> *The subtle, pure, and inmost spirit of life!*
> *My God! I never knew what the mad felt*
> *Before; for I am mad beyond all doubt!*
> (More wildly) *No, I am dead! These putrefying limbs*
> *Shut round and sepulchre the panting soul*
> *Which would burst forth into the wandering air!*

There is worse ranting in Elizabethan drama, even in Webster. But we have only to compare the speeches of Shelley's Beatrice with those of Shakespeare's Isabella to see the difference between a literary conception of character and the lively representation of a human being. However justified the conventions of art may be, they must never contradict the purpose of a particular art-form, and the purpose of drama is, as Shelley realised, fundamentally realistic; it depends on the possibility of the audience participating in the emotional life of the characters. But this will never be achieved by merely negative precautions. "I have avoided with great care in writing this play the introduction of what is commonly called mere poetry. . . . I have written . . . without an over-fastidious and learned choice of words . . . the real language of men in general . . ." Thus Shelley may protest his good intentions, but he is once again really apologising for his impetuosity; and in stripping that impetuosity of its concordant imagery, he was merely reducing the quality without restraining the quantity of his mode of expression. He was being unnatural, and when he had written *Epipsychidion*, the most natural expression of his genius that he ever gave, he realised it. "The *Epipsychidion*," he wrote to John Gisborne, "is a mystery; as to real flesh and blood, you know that I do not deal in those articles; you might as well go to a gin-shop for a leg of mutton, as expect anything human or earthly from me."

That is the basis upon which I shall attempt to justify the poetry of Shelley—not condemn it as failing to achieve something which was not in the nature of the poet, but praise it for expressing, with an unsurpassed perfection, qualities which belonged to the poet and which are of peculiar value to humanity. But first I think it is necessary to establish the psychological type to which Shelley belonged.

III

Anything like an exact psychological analysis of a poet who lived more than a hundred years ago is beyond the scope of literary criticism. The psychologist, on the basis of many anecdotes of his life, by a careful examination and classification of the imagery of his poetry, might be able to arrive at some definite conclusions. But for our present purpose it will be sufficient to establish certain general characteristics, and a knowledge of these may at least save us from the fatuity of blaming the poet for not possessing what it was not in his nature to possess.

If Shelley's life and writings are glanced at with a psychological eye, three significant features will at once be noticed:

(1) the occurrence, at intervals, of hallucinations of a morbid or pathological nature;

(2) an abnormal interest in incest motives;

(3) a general lack of objectivity in his normal mode of self-expression.

The psychologist will immediately form the hypothesis that all these features are related to a common cause, and he will seek to explain them by a general theory of the poet's personality and psychological development. We will first state the facts.

Shelley's liability to sudden and somewhat devastating hallucinations is attested by several of his contemporaries, but most clearly, and with some awareness of their significance, by his intimate friend Thomas Love Peacock. The first attack is fully recorded by Harriet Shelley, in a letter to Hogg dated 12th March, 1813:

"On the night of the 26th February we retired to bed between ten and eleven o'clock. We had been in bed about half an hour, when Mr. S—— heard a noise proceeding from one of the parlours. He immediately went downstairs with two pistols which he had loaded that night, expecting to have occasion for them. He went into the billiard-room, when he heard footsteps retreating; he followed into another little room, which was called an office. He there saw a man in the act of quitting the room through a glass window which opened into the shrubbery; the man fired at Mr. S——, which he avoided. Bysshe then fired, but it flashed in the pan. The man then knocked Bysshe down, and they struggled on the ground. Bysshe then fired his second pistol, which he thought wounded him in his shoulder, as he uttered a shriek and got up, when he said these words: 'By God, I will be revenged. I will murder your wife, and will ravish your sister! By God, I will be revenged!' He then fled, as we hoped for the night. Our servants were not gone to bed, but were just going when this horrible affair happened. This was about eleven o'clock. We all assembled in the parlour, where we remained for two hours. Mr. S—— then advised us to retire, thinking it was impossible he would make a second attack. We left Bysshe and our man-servant—who had only arrived that day, and who knew nothing of the house—to sit up. I had been in bed three hours when I heard a pistol go off. I immediately ran downstairs, when I perceived that Bysshe's flannel gown had been shot through, and the window-curtain. Bysshe had sent Daniel to see what hour it was, when he heard a noise at the window; he went there, and a man thrust his arm through the glass and fired at him. Thank heaven! the ball went through his gown and he remained unhurt. Mr. S—— happened to stand sideways; had he stood fronting, the ball must have killed him. Bysshe fired his pistol, but it would not go off; he then aimed a blow at him with an old sword which we found in the house. The assassin attempted to get the sword from him, and just as he was pulling it away Dan rushed into the room, when he made his escape. This was at four in the morning. It had been a most dreadful night; the wind was as loud as thunder, and the rain descended in torrents. Nothing has been heard of him, and we have every reason to believe it was no stranger, as there is a man . . . who, the next morning, went and told the shopkeepers that it was a tale of Mr. Shelley's to impose upon them, that he might leave the country without paying his bills. This they believed, and none of them attempted to do anything towards the discovery. We left Tanyrallt on Sunday."

This narrative would not survive present scrutiny, for it is full of highly suspicious circumstances. But its genuineness was suspected at the time, and Peacock himself made an investigation. "I was in North Wales in the summer of 1813," he relates, "and heard the matter much talked of. Persons who had examined the premises on the following morning had found that the grass of the lawn appeared to have been much trampled and rolled on, but there were no footmarks on the wet ground, except between the beaten spot and the window; and the impression of the ball on the wainscot showed that the pistol had been fired towards the window, and not from it. This appeared conclusive as to the whole series of operations having taken place from within." That Peacock realised the nature of the hallucination is shown by the comment which follows: "The mental phenomena in which this sort of semi-delusion originated will be better illustrated by one which occurred at a later period, and which, though less tragical in its appearances, was more circumstantial in its development, and more perseveringly adhered to."

Of this later affair, Peacock himself was a witness:

"In the early summer of 1816 the spirit of restlessness again came over him, and resulted in a second visit to the Continent. The change of scene was preceded, as more than once before, by a mysterious communication from a person seen only by himself, warning him of immediate personal perils to be incurred by him if he did not instantly depart.

"I was alone at Bishopgate, with him and Mrs. Shelley, when the visitation alluded to occurred. About the middle of the day, intending to take a walk, I went into the hall for my hat. His was there, and mine was not. I could not imagine what had become of it; but as I could not walk without it, I returned to the library. After some time had elapsed, Mrs. Shelley came in, and gave me an account which she had just received from himself, of the visitor and his communication. I expressed some scepticism on the subject, on which she left me, and Shelley came in, with my hat in his hand. He said: 'Mary tells me, you do not believe that I have had a visit from Williams.' I said: 'I told her there were some improbabilities in the narration.' He said: 'You know Williams of Tremadoc?' I said: 'I do.' He said: 'It was he who was here to-day. He came to tell me of a plot laid by my father and uncle, to entrap me and lock me up. He was in great haste, and could not stop a minute, and I walked with him to Egham.' I said: 'What hat did you wear?' He said: 'This, to be sure.' I said: 'I wish you would put it on.' He put

31

it on, and it went over his face. I said: 'You could
not have walked to Egham in that hat.' He said:
'I snatched it up hastily, and perhaps I kept it in
my hand. I certainly walked with Williams to
Egham, and he told me what I have said. You are
very sceptical.' I said: 'If you are certain of what
you say, my scepticism cannot affect your cer-
tainty.' He said: 'It is very hard on a man who
has devoted his life to the pursuit of truth, who has
made great sacrifices and incurred great sufferings
for it, to be treated as a visionary. If I do not know
that I saw Williams, how do I know that I see
you?' I said: 'An idea may have a force of a
sensation; but the oftener a sensation is repeated,
the greater is the probability of its origin in reality.
You saw me yesterday, and will see me to-morrow.'
He said: 'I can see Williams to-morrow if I please.
He told me that he was stopping at the Turk's
Head Coffee-house, in the Strand, and should be
there two days. I want to convince you that I am
not under a delusion. Will you walk with me to
London to-morrow, to see him?' I said: 'I would
most willingly do so.' The next morning after an
early breakfast we set off on our walk to London.
We had got half way down Egham Hill, when he
suddenly turned round, and said to me: 'I do not
think we shall find Williams at the Turk's Head.'
I said: 'Neither do I.' He said: 'You say that,
because you do not think he has been there; but he
mentioned a contingency under which he might
leave town yesterday, and he has probably done

32

so.' I said: 'At any rate, we should know that he has been there.' He said: 'I will take other means of convincing you. I will write to him. Suppose we take a walk through the forest.' We turned about on our new direction, and were out all day. Some days passed, and I heard no more of the matter. One morning he said to me: 'I have some news of Williams; a letter and an enclosure.' I said: 'I shall be glad to see the letter.' He said: 'I cannot show you the letter; I will show you the enclosure. It is a diamond necklace. I think you know me well enough to be sure I would not throw away my own money on such a thing, and that if I have it, it must have been sent me by somebody else. It has been sent me by Williams.' 'For what purpose?' I asked. He said: 'To prove his identity and his sincerity.' 'Surely,' I said, 'your showing me a diamond necklace will prove nothing but that you have one to show.' 'Then,' he said, 'I will not show it you. If you will not believe me, I must submit to your incredulity.' There the matter ended. I never heard another word of Williams, nor of any other mysterious visitor. I had on one or two previous occasions argued with him against similar semi-delusions, and I believe if they had always been received with similar scepticism, they would not have been often repeated; but they were encouraged by the ready credulity with which they were received by many who ought to have known better. I call them semi-delusions, because for the most part, they had their basis in his firm belief

33

that his father and uncle had designs on his liberty. On this basis his imagination built a fabric of romance, and when he presented it as substantive fact, and it was found to contain more or less of inconsistency, he felt his self-esteem interested in maintaining it by accumulated circumstances, which severally vanished under the touch of investigation, like Williams's location at the Turk's Head Coffee-house.

"I must add that, in the expression of these differences, there was not a shadow of anger. They were discussed with freedom and calmness; with the good temper and good feeling which never forsook him in conversations with his friends. There was an evident anxiety for acquiescence, but a quiet and gentle toleration of dissent."

Delusions of persecution pursued Shelley to Italy. There is a story, which dates from 1818, of his having been knocked down in the post office at Florence by a man in a military cloak, who had suddenly walked up to him, saying: "Are you the damned atheist Shelley?" This man was not seen by anyone else, nor ever afterwards seen or heard of; and Peacock classes this incident with the previous "semi-delusions." In 1822, the year of his death, the hallucinations recurred with unusual intensity. In June Shelley was busy writing *The Triumph of Life*. The composition of this poem, the perpetual presence of the sea, and other causes, relates Lady Shelley:

"contributed to plunge the mind of Shelley into a

state of morbid excitement, the result of which was a tendency to see visions. One night loud cries were heard issuing from the saloon. The Williamses rushed out of their room in alarm; Mrs. Shelley also endeavoured to reach the spot, but fainted at the door. Entering the saloon, the Williamses found Shelley staring horribly into the air, and evidently in a trance. They waked him, and he related that a figure wrapped in a mantle came to his bedside and beckoned him. He must then have risen in his sleep, for he followed the imaginary figure into the saloon, when it lifted the hood of its mantle, ejaculated 'Siete sodisfatto?' and vanished."

Another vision which occurred about this time is recorded by Williams in his diary published in Lady Shelley's *Shelley Memorials*:

"May 6. Fine. Some heavy drops of rain fell without a cloud being visible. After tea, while walking with Shelley on the terrace, and observing the effect of moonshine on the waters, he complained of being unusually nervous, and, stopping short, he grasped me violently by the arm, and stared steadfastly on the white surf that broke upon the beach under our feet. Observing him sensibly affected, I demanded of him if he was in pain; but he only answered by saying: 'There it is again! there!' He recovered after some time, and declared that he saw, as plainly as he then saw me, a naked child (Allegra, who had recently died) rise from the sea, and clasp its hands as if in joy, smiling at him. This was a trance that it required some reasoning and philosophy entirely to wake him from, so forcibly had the vision operated on his mind."

It is possible that this last vision is of a somewhat different type from the rest, but the evidence as a whole is sufficient to establish the fact that Shelley was suffering, during the last ten years of his life (and therefore during the whole of his effective poetic period) from a well-established kind of psychosis,* the "paranoid" type of dementia præcox. Any further description of this psychological abnormality is not necessary—its character is sufficiently evident in the case presented by Shelley. We must now investigate the possible cause of the psychosis, but first I must describe the other significant features in Shelley's make-up.

Shelley's first attempt to deal openly with the incest motive was made in 1817, when he wrote *Laon and Cythna*, the original version of *The Revolt of Islam*. The poem was actually set up, and a few copies printed, before the publisher, Ollier, discovered that the lovers Laon and Cythna were represented as brother and sister. He was horrified and hastily stopped the publication, and then insisted on the poem being amended. Shelley put up the strongest resistance, but Ollier remained firm, so finally Shelley submitted, and the poem, with a few

* In general I have preferred to use the term "psychosis" rather than "neurosis," following the distinction made by Freud. [*Collected Papers*, Vol. II.]

changes of sex, appeared as *The Revolt of Islam.*
Undismayed by this experience, Shelley two years
later returned to the theme in *The Cenci,* the work by
which he is perhaps still best known. As Shelley was
at pains to point out, it was the facts of the story
which interested him, and which he proposed to
present, abating the horror in an idealisation of the
characters, without any attempt to make them
"subservient to what is vulgarly termed a moral
purpose." For the present merely the fact that in two
of his major works Shelley took incest as a motive is
significant for our enquiry into his psychosis.

The third feature I mentioned, the general lack of
objectivity in Shelley's mode of self-expression, is one
which has its poetic as well as its psychological interest. But for the moment I confine myself to the
latter aspect. It is a commonplace observation that
most people's senses are unbalanced; one person will
have keen visual sensibility, another keen aural sensibility; in others the sense of touch or smell will be developed at the expense of the rest of the senses. "When
I first knew Shelley," Hogg writes, "he was alike indifferent to all works of art. He learned afterwards to
admire statues, and then, at a still later period, pictures; but he never had any feeling for the wonders of
architecture; even our majestic cathedrals were
viewed with indifference. I took him into York Min-
ster several times, but to no purpose; it was thrown
away, entirely lost upon him. The insensible Harriet
appeared to feel its beauty, until her admiration of
the sublime structure was proscribed and forbidden

37

by authority." That Hogg was not in this matter in any way misrepresenting Shelley is shown by those very reactions to statues and pictures which Hogg refers to, and which still survive in Shelley's letters from Italy, and in his "Critical Notices of the Sculpture in the Florence Gallery." Most art criticism of the period is "literary," but Shelley's notes show a complete unawareness of anything in the nature of what we should now call plastic values. A passage from a letter to Leigh Hunt (Sept. 8th, 1918) will serve as an illustration:

"Perhaps I attended more to sculpture than to painting, its forms being more easily intelligible than that of the latter. Yet, I saw the famous works of Raffaele, whom I agree with the whole world in thinking the finest painter. With respect to Michael Angelo I dissent, and think with astonishment and indignation of the common notion that he equals, and, in some respects, exceeds Raffaele. He seems to me to have no sense of moral dignity and loveliness; and the energy for which he has been so much praised, appears to me to be a certain rude, external, mechanical quality, in comparison with anything possessed by Raffaele, or even much inferior artists. His famous painting in the Sixtine Chapel seems to me deficient in beauty and majesty, both in the conception and the execution. He has been called the Dante of painting; but if we find some of the gross and strong outlines which are employed in the most distasteful passages of the *Inferno*, where shall we find *your* Francesca—where the spirit coming over the sea in a boat, like Mars rising from the vapours of the horizon—where Matilda gathering flowers, and all the exquisite tenderness, and sensibility, and ideal beauty, in which Dante excelled all poets except Shakespeare."

In a letter to Peacock on the same subject, Shelley is even more outspoken about Michelangelo. "He has not only no temperance, no modesty, no feeling for the just boundaries of art. . . . but he has no sense of beauty, and to want this is to want the sense of the creative power of mind." The odd thing is, that Shelley accuses Michelangelo of lacking precisely those qualities which a modern critic would see in the sculptor: majesty, creative power, moral dignity, idealisation of the human type. One cannot help feeling that some other quality in the artist repelled Shelley—perhaps his extreme masculinity, which Shelley designated as "a certain rude, external, mechanical quality"; or perhaps still obscurer aspects of Michelangelo's homosexuality.

It happens that a certain modern psychological theory will account for all these features in Shelley's personality, and though this theory will meet with a good deal of resistance, particularly from friends of Shelley, and will therefore seem very inappropriate to a so-called defence of Shelley, I shall put it forward, since I believe that the knowledge which comes from a complete understanding of a poet's personality is the best basis for the appreciation of his poetry. For it is not a belief in the ideas or dogmas of a poet that is essential for the reader's poetic "assent," but rather a sympathy with his personality; and this is the sense in which I wish to amend Mr. Eliot's amendment of Dr. Richards's amendment of Coleridge's original suggestion.

The psychological theory I have in mind, known as "the principle of primary identification," was first put forward by Dr. Trigant Burrow in two papers contributed to *The Psychoanalytical Review*;* there is an accessible discussion of it in Chapter XVI of Dr. John T. MacCurdy's *Problems in Dynamic Psychology*.† It is a theory which attempts to explain the origin of homosexual tendencies, and the consequences of the suppression of these tendencies, and as Dr. MacCurdy says, "it is peculiarly significant that this, the most original and important contribution to psychoanalysis of recent years, has received no attention from Freud and his immediate followers." I cannot do better than quote the summary of this theory as given by MacCurdy:

"While still *in utero*, the infant's 'organic consciousness is so harmoniously adapted to its environment as to constitute a perfect continuum with it.' The fœtus has no knowledge of where he begins and the maternal envelope ends. He has no personality,

*The Genesis and Meaning of Homosexuality and its Relation to the Problem of Introverted Mental States (Vol. 4, no. 3) and The Origin of the Incest-Awe (Vol. 5, no. 3).

†Cambridge University Press, 1923. Quoted with the kind permission of the Syndics.

no individuality, because these are the sum of consistent reactions to the environment which give the organism its psychic individuality or personality. Even for some months after birth the child is still without true individuality and, so far as consciousness is concerned, is still an extension of the mother, so to speak, for all his experience is gained through or with the mother.

" 'Now during these early months of the infant's exclusive relationship with the mother, organic associations begin to be formed which mark the beginning of the awakening of consciousness. Let it be remembered though that since the child is still in the subjective, undifferentiated phase of consciousness, the associations of the first months of infantile life are entirely primary, subjective and unconscious, and that therefore its early associations, being subjective, non-conscious and undifferentiated, tend always toward the closer consolidation of the mother with itself, that is to say, they tend to the indissoluble welding together of the infantile ego and the mother-image. Thus is strengthened from day to day the mental union— the psychic amalgamation between the mother and infant which establishes for him an organic bond in respect to feeling or consciousness subsequent to birth that is correlative with the organic correspondence prior to their separation at birth. It is his subjective continuity—this organic mental bond —which I call the *principle of primary identification*.'

". . . Such consciousness as [the infant] does enjoy

is the subjective unity with his mother, hence his first efforts at objectivation follow the line of his mother's solicitation, namely, himself. So he regards his own body as a love-object, just as does his mother. With weaning he is thrown more back upon himself and his body becomes the constant and insistent object of his interest. Thus auto-erotism. *'Now auto-erotism or the love of one's own body is the love of that sex to which one's own body belongs and this, in psychological interpretation, is precisely homosexuality.'*

"By this argument unconscious homosexuality is merely an extension into adult life of the primary identification, and a psychoneurosis a state of heightened subjectivity correlated with the unconscious homosexuality which is simply one expression of it.

". . . [Burrow] proceeds to examine the 'sentiment of love' and finds that it consists in identification with the love-object. It is not hard to find evidence of the existence of this factor and Burrow adduces many examples from the vocabulary of love to prove it. Normally the biological sex urge leads the individual to direct his love capacity, his identification tendency, to one of the opposite sex, but the neurotic is so dominated by the primary identification that he cannot do this and so tends to identify himself, unconsciously at least, with one like himself, i.e., he is homosexual.

"Unconscious homosexuality is thus merely incidental to the psychoneurosis. A much more fundamental problem is the origin of repression, without which one would not get all the distortions and evasions which constitute symptoms. Repression in general is typified in the horror, the revolt, against incest, so Burrow sets himself to the task of relating this to his principle of primary identification."

This outline is perhaps sufficient for our purpose, but there are some detailed consequences of the theory which fit in with the case of Shelley. For example, in describing the process of adaptation, Dr. Burrow explains how it comes about that some individuals, and precisely those who do not succeed in completely adapting themselves, will show a lack of objectivity.

"Now the demands of the world of outer objectivity or of consciousness proper entail increasing outrage to this state of primary quiescence. . . . Thus our primary nature shrinks from the intrusion of those outer impressions which disturb its elemental sleep. And so it may be said that *Nature abhors consciousness.* But with the increasing importunities of reality there begins the gradual increase of outer objective consciousness. Slowly there is the establishment of that *rapport* between the organism and the external world, which constitutes individual adaptation. Observe that the process of adaptation is essentially outward-tending, away from the ego, that it is inherently a process of objectivation."

It would follow, therefore, that a poet who had not successfully adapted himself to the external world, who was, at least unconsciously, still firmly bound to that state of consciousness which succeeds the primary identification with the mother—who was, that is to say, unconsciously homosexual—would be distinguished by a lack of objectivity in his attitude towards the outer world, and in his description of that attitude, that is to say, in his poetic diction. And such is precisely the character of Shelley's poetry.

A psychologist would probably be inclined to ask for more specific evidence of unconscious homosexuality in the actual imagery used by Shelley. I think enough to satisfy the psychologist could be found in Shelley's works—abundantly in the two prose romances, for example, which were his first published works, and even in his most deliberate poems, such as *Adonais*.* But any such research I

*The symbol of the Eagle and the Serpent is a typical example of the kind of imagery that calls for some psychological explanation. It is used no less than four times by Shelley—in *Alastor*, ll. 227–237; ll. 324–5; *Prometheus Unbound*, III, ii, 72–4; and with great elaboration in Canto I of *The Revolt of Islam*:

> *For in the air do I behold indeed*
> *An Eagle and a Serpent wreathed in fight:—*
> *And now relaxing its impetuous flight,*
> *Before the aëreal rock on which I stood,*
> *The Eagle, hovering, wheeled to left and right,*
> *And hung with lingering wings over the flood,*
> *And startled with its yells the wide air's solitude.*
>
> *A shaft of light upon its wings descended,*
> *And every golden feather gleamed therein—*
> *Feather and scale, inextricably blended.*
> *The Serpent's mailed and many-coloured skin*
> *Shone through the plumes its coils were twined within*
> *By many a swoln and knotted fold, and high*
> *And far, the neck, receding lithe and thin,*
> *Sustained a crested head, which warily*
> *Shifted and glanced before the Eagle's steadfast eye.*

44

must leave to the psychologist. I would, however, like to point to the significance of a passage in one of Shelley's incompleted prose works, his *Speculations on Metaphysics*, the fifth section of which is an extraordinary anticipation of psychoanalysis. "Let us reflect on our infancy," begins Shelley, "and give as faithfully as possible a relation of the events of sleep." And then he proceeds to give "a faithful picture of my own peculiar nature relatively to sleep."

"I distinctly remember dreaming three several times, between intervals of two or more years, the same precise dream. It was not so much what is ordinarily called a dream; the single image, unconnected with all other images, of a youth who was educated at the same school with myself, presented itself in sleep. Even now, after the lapse of many years, I can never hear the name of this

> Around, around, in ceaseless circles wheeling
>   With clang of wings and scream, the Eagle sailed
> Incessantly—sometimes on high concealing
>   Its lessening orbs, sometimes as if it failed,
>   Drooped through the air; and still it shrieked and wailed,
> And casting back its eager head, with beak
>   And talon unremittingly assailed
> The wreathèd Serpent, who did ever seek
> Upon his enemy's heart a mortal wound to wreak.

>   . . . in the void air, far away,
>   Floated the shattered plumes; bright scales did leap,
> Where'er the Eagle's talons made their way,
> Like sparks into the darkness;—as they sweep,
> Blood stains the snowy foam of the tumultuous deep.

The description of the struggle continues for three more stanzas, and then the Eagle drops the Serpent, which falls to the sea, and makes its way to where a Woman, beautiful as morning, sits beneath the rocks. When the Woman sees the Serpent, she breaks into song—"his native tongue and hers"—

45

youth, without the three places where I dreamed
of him presenting themselves to my mind . . .

"I have beheld scenes, with the intimate and un-
accountable connexion of which with the obscure
parts of my own nature, I have been irresistibly
impressed. I have beheld a scene which has produced no unusual effect on my thoughts. After the
lapse of many years I have dreamed of this scene.
It has hung on my memory, it has haunted my
thoughts, at intervals, with the pertinacity of an
object connected with human affections. I have
visited this scene again. Neither the dream could
be dissociated from the landscape, nor the landscape from the dream, nor feelings, such as neither
singly could have awakened, from both. But the
most remarkable event of this nature, which ever
occurred to me, happened five years ago at Oxford.
I was walking with a friend, in the neighbourhood

And she unveiled her bosom, and the green
And glancing shadows of the sea did play
O'er its marmoreal depth: —one moment seen,
For ere the next, the Serpent did obey
Her voice, and, coiled in rest in her embrace it lay.

Possibly the psychologist will recognise in this imagery an archetypal
pattern for which he has a ready interpretation—most probably some
form of castration complex.* An eagle grasping a serpent is, of course,
an emblem of fairly frequent occurrence; Mr. Hugh Sykes Davies
tells me that the image is used by Homer. It is possible, therefore, that
Shelley consciously selected it; but what is of significance is not so much
the selection of the image, as the extraordinary vividness and detail
which it assumes in Shelley's relation. Those qualities, we may assume,
had a powerful subconscious motivation; and since this passage is one
of Shelley's high poetic achievements, we are entitled to look for
psychological explanations of all hyperæsthetic expression. There could
be no clearer justification, if any were needed, of the psychological
method in literary criticism.

*Cf. The Riddle of the Sphinx, by Géza Róheim. (London: Hogarth
Press, 1934.)

of that city, engaged in earnest and interesting conversation. We suddenly turned the corner of a lane, and the view, which its high banks and hedges had concealed, presented itself. The view consisted of a windmill, standing in one among many plashy meadows, inclosed with stone walls; the irregular and broken ground, between the wall and the road on which we stood; a long low hill behind the windmill, and a grey covering of uniform cloud spread over the sky. It was that season when the last leaf had just fallen from the scant and stunted ash. The scene surely was a common scene; the season and the hour little calculated *to kindle lawless thought;* it was a tame uninteresting assemblage of objects, such as would drive the imagination for refuge in serious and sober talk, to the evening fireside, and the dessert of winter fruits and wine. The effect which it produced on me was not such as could have been expected. I suddenly remembered to have seen that exact scene in some dream of long . . ."

The account breaks off thus abruptly, and Shelley adds in a note:

"Here I was obliged to leave off, *overcome by thrilling horror.*"

We shall never know what "thrilling horror," what "lawless thought," was present in such vividness in Shelley's dream that he could not bring himself to relate the incident. We can only speculate that it was a scene connected with that "horror" which had such a strong and inexplicable fascination for him—the horror of incest. Lest it be thought that a horror of incest would be inconsistent with the open treatment of the theme such as we get in *The Cenci*, here is a statement from MacCurdy, made without reference to Shelley, but in general reference to the kind of psychosis Shelley seems to have suffered from: "According to Burrow's thesis, such an individual should have the greatest repugnance to incest and show the greatest capacity for 'love.' Yet he can entertain delusions of incest without evidence of any horror at the thought and is less capable of love, as that term is usually understood, than any other clinical type we know about."

This brings us to the final evidence for assuming that Shelley lived in a state of heightened subjectivity due to his unconscious homosexuality—his attitude to love. We shall still rely on the psychology of Burrow, which provides us with a very satisfactory explanation of two types of love with which Shelley was much concerned. Love, in this psychology, is closely identified with that striving for unity which is the normal unconscious effort of the individual. In the individual who is fully adapted to his social environment, the normal individual who has completely repressed the desire for unity and can enter into objective sexual relations with another individual of the opposite sex on a basis of reciprocity and partnership. But in the case of the incompletely adapted individual, his essential subjectivity will demand a more generalised kind of unity, in which there is no separation of the individual from the world at large. Subjectivity implies a lack of interest in one's environment, and a consequent longing for community of thinking. To quote Burrow:

> "It is but natural that having come suddenly into the franchise of consciousness, man should employ his liberty of action in the wanton aims of personal satisfaction, or in the tedious propitiations of vicarious conformities. But there is something deeper still, more native to man, than all this. It is expressed in the social merging of personalities into each other in the pursuit of the common good. It is that quality of man that ever goads him to search and strive to the utmost benefit of the race. It is this quality of harmoniousness and unity inherent in the social aims of man that is, it seems to me, the strongest principle of man's consciousness. This it is that men have called love. This, it seems to me, is the true affirmation of life and its prototype is the harmonious principle of the preconscious."

That this theory corresponds in general to Shelley's attitude to the subject will be at once obvious. But the extraordinary completeness with which Shelley expresses the view that we should, according to our hypothesis, expect him to express, can only be demonstrated by further quotation. The *Epipsy-*

chidion is, of course, the supreme expression of his
philosophy, and there could be no better instance
of how some understanding of the psychology of a
poet can aid us to an appreciation of his poetry;
and of how for the lack of such understanding so
sensitive a reader of poetry as Mr. Eliot can be
"thoroughly gravelled." The lines which troubled
Mr. Eliot and which he quotes in his lecture, restored
to their proper order and the omitted lines added,
are these:

> *I never was attached to that great sect,*
> *Whose doctrine is, that each one should select*
> *Out of the crowd a mistress or a friend,*
> *And all the rest, though fair and wise, commend*
> *To cold oblivion, though it is the code*
> *Of modern morals, and the beaten road*
> *Which those poor slaves with weary footsteps tread,*
> *Who travel to their home among the dead*
> *By the broad highway of the world, and so*
> *With one chained friend, perhaps a jealous foe,*
> *The dreariest and the longest journey go.*
>
> *True Love in this differs from gold and clay,*
> *That to divide is not to take away.*
> *Love is like understanding, that grows bright,*
> *Gazing on many truths; 'tis like thy light,*
> *Imagination! which from earth and sky,*
> *And from the depths of human fantasy,*
> *As from a thousand prisms and mirrors, fills*
> *The Universe with glorious beams, and kills*

Error, the worm, with many a sun-like arrow
Of its reverberated lightning. Narrow
The heart that loves, the brain that contemplates,
The life that wears, the spirit that creates
One object, and one form, and builds thereby
A sepulchre for its eternity.

There is nothing, I would submit, in such a poetic statement, to gravel any unprejudiced reader; the doctrine is clear and coherent, and, as I am attempting to show, based on—indeed, a consequence of—psychological realities. The question of the "normality" of these realities I will deal with presently; but first, to present Shelley's doctrine in all its clarity, I must quote a prose statement which he wrote in 1815:

> "*Thou* demandest what is love? It is that powerful attraction towards all that we conceive, or fear, or hope beyond ourselves, when we find within our own thoughts the chasm of an insufficient void, and seek to awaken in all things that are, a community with what we experience within ourselves. If we reason, we would be understood; if we imagine, we would that the airy children of our brain were born anew within another's; if we feel, we would that another's nerves should vibrate to our own, that the beams of their eyes should kindle at once and mix and melt into our own, that lips of motionless ice should not reply to lips quivering and burning with the heart's best blood.

This is Love. This is the bond and the sanction
which connects not only man with man, but with
everything which exists. We are born into the
world, and there is something within us which,
from the instant that we live, more and more
thirsts after its likeness. It is probably in correspondence with this law that the infant drains milk
from the bosom of its mother; this propensity
develops itself with the development of our nature.
We dimly see within our intellectual nature a
miniature as it were of our entire self, yet deprived
of all that we condemn or despise, the ideal prototype of everything excellent or lovely that we are
capable of conceiving as belonging to the nature
of man. Not only the portrait of our external being,
but an assemblage of the minutest particles of
which our nature is composed;* a mirror whose
surface reflects only the forms of purity and brightness; a soul within our soul that describes a circle
around its proper paradise, which pain, and
sorrow, and evil dare not overleap. To this we
eagerly refer all sensations, thirsting that they
should resemble or correspond with it. The discovery of its antitype; the meeting with an understanding capable of clearly estimating our own;
an imagination which should enter into and seize
upon the subtle and delicate peculiarities which
we have delighted to cherish and unfold in secret;
with a frame whose nerves, like the chords of two

---

*These words are ineffectual and metaphorical. Most words are so—
No help! (Shelley's note.)

exquisite lyres, strung to the accompaniment of
one delightful voice, vibrate with the vibrations of
our own; and of a combination of all these in such
proportion as the type within demands; this is the
invisible and unattainable point to which Love
tends; and to attain which, it urges forth the powers
of man to arrest the faintest shadow of that, without the possession of which there is no rest nor
respite to the heart over which it rules."

Here, in language which only differs from a modern
psychologist's in being poetic rather than technical,
we have a clear description of the state of narcissism,
that stage in the development of the individual when
a growing self-consciousness becomes a growing self-
love. Physically this state may be expressed in auto-
erotic practices, but it can exist without auto-erotism,
in fantasy alone. From narcissism the individual
develops towards homosexuality (love of another
like oneself) or towards heterosexuality, where
objectivity may be completely developed. But, in
Dr. MacCurdy's words, "very frequently the alleged
object of love is merely a lay figure; the subject is
in love with his ideal of what the loved one should
be. In such a case the union is happy just in so far
as the object of attachment is capable of identifying
himself or herself with the ideal. This type of love
is narcissistic because what is loved is not another
person at all but an autochthonous ideal. True
objectivity occurs only when another person is loved
as another personality and not only in so far as the

object duplicates a fantasy of the lover. When a sexual object is credited with undue virtue (sexual overestimation), this is a product of narcissism, because the qualities in question do not reside in the object (or not in the degree represented) but are fantasies of the lover, things he would like to see and, therefore, does observe. Such an attachment may pass for true love, thanks to its loud protestations, but it is unstable. A puff of reality will blow it away." It will at once be obvious how closely Shelley's love affairs correspond to this description. Not only in his explicit ideas, but in the actions of his life, he reveals himself as a narcissistic type.

This, I think, is about as far as the literary critic can carry the psychological analysis of a poet. It has enabled us to establish beyond any reasonable doubt that Shelley belonged to a definite psychological type—a type whose consciousness is incompletely objectified, which is therefore evidently narcissistic, and unconsciously homosexual. Such unconscious homosexuality gives rise to a psychosis of which Shelley shows all the normal symptoms. It determines a line of moral conduct which Shelley exhibits in his life. It determines a quality of imagery and verbal expression which is present in Shelley's verse. It has as its concomitant a unity-complex which leads to the development of those social ideas of a communist tendency which are characteristic of Shelley's political thought. The chain of evidence is complete; it does not, so far as I can see, leave any room for argument.

But what still remains to be done is to give some estimate of the value of such a type. And by "value" I mean the worth of such an individual to the social and intellectual life of the community at large. For it cannot be assumed that what is not normal is not valuable.

IV

Giebt es vielleicht—eine Frage für Irren-
ärtze—Neurosen der Gesundheit?
NIETZSCHE.

One thing which modern psychology may claim to have established beyond question is the relativity of all human types; at least, the psychologist will tell you that any preconceived idea of normality will break down on the most superficial analysis. Dr. Burrow has called normality "unconsciousness on a co-operative basis," and he for one is not deceived by the compromise it represents. But if not a reality in any absolute sense, this co-operative basis is an accepted fiction or illusion from which the neurotic finds himself excluded. The values of the actual situation are majority values—the conventional values of morality, conduct and taste. There is no evidence whatever that such values are, in any positive sense, biological or organic values—by which I mean values which promote the health and happiness of mankind in the only world of which we have any certain knowledge. If one is strong enough to detach one's self from the normal assumptions of society (thereby becoming, if only for the moment, neurotic), then what, we may ask ourselves, is the value of this normal man—this man who has lost the joy of his childhood; this man who, clad in the triple armour of routine, convention and cant, goes through the paces of his hypocritical day; rising from a sleep in which the baffled forces of life have flickered phantasmagorically behind the screen of consciousness; immediately assuming the common mask, a shaven mask to which adheres, perhaps, a rudimentary whisker; then, having bathed and eased himself in shame-faced privacy, pursuing his daily course, donning his dull traditional clothing, fastening his senseless buttons, his starched collar, his polished boots; greeting his friends with his usual grin; this pipe-sucking busybody, reading his newspaper which panders fulsomely to his unconscious sadism, his repressed homosexuality, his all-pervasive eroticism—need we follow him through the whole round of his visits, avocations and amusements? (Little man, he's had a busy day!) Not one moment of impersonal spontaneity, of whole-hearted participation in a life free, communal and unconfined. Everywhere the taboo, the code, the eternal vigilance of the unknown censor.

Against this mass self-deception, the neurotic is doomed to protest. It may be that in the process of his individual adaptation to life, his growth has been arrested; he has not, that is to say, completely dissociated himself from his original organic unity with his mother. He has not been fully weaned, he has not been completely *won* for society. Forcibly divorced from his mother, all the strength of his feeling has been transferred to the object of his mother's greatest regard—to himself. Social adaptation consists precisely in getting rid of this self-interest, this autosexuality; in sublimating it, as we say. But such adaptation is really a pretence; under the cover of our conventions we remain disparate, dissociated, resisting the organic wholeness of life. Only the neurotic refuses the compromise. Disparate as he may seem from the point of view of the normality we have achieved, actually he is nearer the source of life, the organic reality; his separateness is really an integrity of personality, an agreement of all the instinctive and affective life of the individual with the organic processes of life in general (the natural unity of our common life). "If the neurotic regarded individually, or as the embodiment within himself of a societal lesion," writes Dr. Burrow, "is an expression of separatism and pathology, the neurotic viewed organically, or as the embodiment within himself of the societal continuum, is no less an expression of confluence and health. If, in the first instance, he is himself the disorder that is his own separatism and unconsciousness, in the second he is the integration that is his own confluence and consciousness. It is this constructive aspect of the neuroses of which we have not yet taken account and of which we may take due cognizance only upon the basis of a wider, organismic interpretation of these disorders of the personality."*

Our next step is to correlate, from this point of view, the neurotic and the artist. Actually this has already been done by Dr. Burrow. "The organic integrity of personality that is the composite life of man and that is organically inseparable from the unifying urge embodied in the impulse of mating, has its clearest intimations in the affirmations of the artist as in the frustrations of the neurotic." The artist, that is to say, reveals an inward unity and concentration of personality in marked contrast with the extraneous dissipations and diversities of the average reaction-type: "It is this unity of personality that is the source of the artist's creativeness as it is the inspiration of his genius. This composite quality of the sex life explains the gentler intuitions we often find in the personality of a man. There is undoubtedly the feminine in man though as yet he stands in fear of it. It does not wrangle or contend. It does not calculate success. The feminine in man is the artist in man.† It is because of this that there can be in the societal unity of the artist's intuitive instinct no place for the illusion that is called 'the public.' To him 'the public' is but the collective repudiation of the common soul of man—a repudiation that corresponds to this same disavowal within the private soul of each of us. Unmoved by its clamorous demands, the artist feels within these

*The Social Basis of Unconsciousness, p. 153.

†Cf. Hopkins: ". . . the things must come from the mundus muliebris." Quoted p. 135 below.

manifestations of the public mind the common soul that underlies it, and senses within it the pain of denied needs identical with his own. This is the unfailing intuition of the artist."*

The relevance of these distinctions to the case of Shelley will by now be evident. But before returning to Shelley I would like to refer to my previous discussion, in *Form in Modern Poetry*, of the distinction between personality and character in relation to the poetic process. When I wrote that essay I had not read any of Dr. Burrow's works; I was elaborating certain statements of Keats's, and in so far as I was going beyond my own experience, I was relying on my understanding of Freud. I feel now that the truth I was attempting to formulate is amply confirmed by Dr. Burrow (who was trained in the Freudian school) and given a more scientific basis. Literary critics like Mr. Eliot may refuse to be drawn into this discussion,† but it should now be obvious that such an attitude is merely an avoidance of the essential issue for modern criticism.

To return to Shelley. From the pathological point of view, Shelley was a neurotic, in conflict with the social imposition of normality. But from a more general and human point of view, Shelley was a genius whose neurotic reaction, for all its distortion, represents an organic urge towards "a completer oneness of life," "a clearer, more conscious social

Op. cit., pp. 218–9.
†"Mr. Herbert Read . . . pursues his speculations to a point to which I would not willingly follow him." *The Use of Poetry and the Use of Criticism*, p. 101 n.

order." As much might be said of other poets—of Keats, for example. But just as, in Burrow's words, "it is the distinction of the neurotic personality that he is at least consciously and confessedly *nervous*," so the special value of Shelley is that he was conscious of his direction; he had, in the modern sense, but without expressing himself in modern terminology, analysed his own neurosis. He did not *define* his autosexuality; but he allowed the reaction full scope. That is to say, he allowed his feelings and ideas to develop integrally with his neurotic personality; and the élan of that evolution inevitably led to the formulation of "a clearer, more conscious social order."

In the light of this analysis, therefore, we must reconsider those "shabby ideas" of his. For not for the first time in the history of human thought, the stone which the builders rejected may become the head of the corner.

<h1 style="text-align:center">V</h1>

It is not part of my intention in this essay to give any extensive account of Shelley's political and moral ideas; that has often been done before, most recently by Mr. John Shawcross in his Introduction to a selection of *Shelley's Literary and Philosophical Criticism* published in the Oxford Miscellany in 1909. But it is necessary to say something in answer to the charge of incoherence, for that, as we have seen, is the main clause in Mr. Eliot's indictment.

Any intelligent mind, during the period of development or formation (a period which, in the most intelligent minds, lasts as long as life), is open to two kinds of influence. One is immediate, and is concerned with the temporary problems of the age we live in; the other is less urgent but more enduring, and is concerned with the permanent problems of human destiny. It is possible to adopt a superior attitude, and say that all the problems that matter were solved once and for all time by Aristotle, or by St. Thomas, or by Kant; and that all we need do at any particular stage of history is to apply the eternal principles of one or other of these philosophers. It is a possible attitude but not a very helpful one; it involves the dogmatist in casuistry, for the immediate problems in life are not necessarily the permanent ones. In our own day we shall look in vain to the past for any solution of the peculiar problems, ethical as well as economic, introduced into our society by modern industrial and scientific methods of production. We are likely to find more guidance in the works of Freud and Marx. It would be equally foolish to seek the source of all wisdom in contemporary philosophers, for wisdom, unfortunately, is not cumulative. It is an insight given to but few individuals in the course of history; and when not faced by new factors, we do well to hold on to the truths tested by universal experience.

From the point of view of the present day, all this is very obvious, if not platitudinous. But when we are considering a poet of another age, such as Shelley, we do not necessarily bear this distinction in mind. We can, if we are not sympathetic, judge him by his immediate influences—the enthusiasms called forth by the urgent problems of his age—and ignore the fact that he was equally influenced by forces we readily accept as valid for all time. The only legitimate demand we might make, perhaps, is that the contemporary enthusiasms should not be the only enthusiasms. We justly suspect the mind that feeds exclusively on a diet of raw opinions. We demand balance, if not consistency. But no one, so far as I am aware (certainly none of the critics I have mentioned), has demonstrated even the inconsistency of Shelley's views. There has been plenty of vague assertion, inspired by prejudice, but no proof.

We can trace Shelley's intellectual development with fair ease. He himself, in one of his early letters to Godwin (June 3, 1812), gives us a somewhat picturesque summary: "Until my marriage, my life had been a series of illness; as it was of a nervous and spasmodic nature, it in a degree incapacitated me for study. I nevertheless, in the intervals of comparative health, read romances, and those the most marvellous ones, unremittingly, and pored over the reveries of Albertus Magnus and Paracelsus, the former of which I read in Latin, and probably gained more knowledge of that language from that source than from all the discipline of Eton. My fondness for natural magic and ghosts abated as my age increased. I read Locke, Hume, Reid, and whatever metaphysics came in my way, without, however, renouncing poetry, an attachment to which has characterized all my wanderings and changes. I did not truly *think* and *feel*, however, until I read *Political Justice*, though my thought and feelings, after this period, have been more painful, anxious, and vivid —more inclined to action and less to theory. Before I was a republican: Athens appeared to me the model of government; but afterwards, Athens bore in my mind the same relation to perfection that Great Britain did to Athens." At Oxford (1810-1), we learn from Hogg, Hume's *Essays* was his favourite book; he also studied Locke with great care, and also "certain popular French works that treat of man, for the most part in a mixed method, metaphysically, morally, and politically." It was then that he began to read Plato, and "was vehemently excited by the striking doctrines which Socrates unfolds." From then onwards he read Greek continuously, and became very proficient in the language. "Few were aware," says Hogg, "of the extent, and still fewer of the profundity of his reading; in his short life, and without ostentation, he had, in truth, read more Greek than many an aged pedant. . . . A pocket edition of Plato, of Plutarch, of Euripides, without interpretation or notes, or of the Septuagint, was his ordinary companion; and he read the text straightforward for hours, if not as readily as an English author, at least with as much facility as French, Italian, or Spanish." During the last four years of his life, during the time he was writing his greatest poetry, he read Homer and Plato, Dante and Ariosto, Calderon and Goethe; he read them with continuous pleasure and deep understanding, and from these authors, if from any, he borrowed his shabby ideas.

We might arrange his precursors in three groups: first Plato and other classical writers, such as Lucretius; then the philosophers of the Enlightenment, Locke and Hume, and their more platonic counterparts, Berkeley and Spinoza; and finally that school of philosophical radicalism which begins with Rousseau, includes Helvétius and Condorcet, and ends for Shelley with Godwin. It is possible to say that here we have mutually exclusive elements; there is little sympathy between Plato and Locke, for example. But we are not to imagine that Shelley accepted all these philosophers in equal measure. Plato was his touchstone, and to Plato he could assimilate what was most sympathetic in the others. But he was guided, of course, by his own intuition of the truth. "As a poet and artist," Mr. Shawcross very rightly observes, "Shelley is essentially a lover of order; in order he sees the principle of beauty, whether expressed in sensuous form or civic institution. It is against defective institutions that his attack on society is aimed—defective, because they fail to reflect outwardly the inner moral law."

A captious critic might complain that the phrase I have used, "his intuition of the truth," begs the question of coherence, but I should be willing if necessary to explain such a phrase in psychological terms. For my principle all the time is that an individual's coherence of thought is a reflection of his coherent personality—by which, of course, I do not mean a consistent character. We build our philosophy, our "view of life," round our psychic elements—round our experience, if a plainer but a vaguer expression is preferred. Even Mr. Shawcross, who is innocent of my psychology, notes that "no doubt in Shelley's aversion from the concrete and the complex we must seek an explanation of the remarkable influence which Godwin's writings exercised upon him." In the same psychological facts we must seek an explanation of Plato's influence upon him. We may only be distinguishing between two kinds of philosophy, or, as Shelley expresses it in the first paragraph already quoted from *A Defence of Poetry*, between reason and imagination; but there is absolutely no necessity to regard one kind of logic or consistency (the consistency of a system within itself, the parts with the whole) as infallible, and preferable to another kind of logic (the consistency of a system as an interpretation of the materials of human nature and life). The first may be science and the second allegory; but both may be equally coherent, mature, and founded on the facts of experience.

The precise terms of Shelley's "view of life" are never in doubt. That view may be idealistic, humanitarian and radical, but it is expressed, both in prose and verse, with a clarity which is not normally associated with a muddled mind. The notes to *Queen Mab*, the work of a youth of eighteen, are admirable in style, and show a mastery of exposition and dialectic which would be hard to match among the intellectual prodigies of the world. They deal with a dizzy range of subjects—astronomy, militarism, the labour theory of value, prostitution, the doctrine of necessity, atheism, Christian evidence, time, and vegetarianism. But however diverse the subjects, they are illuminated from one centre: a mind and personality of singular energy, purity and compassion. It was a mind, moreover, that was continually expanding and enriching itself; and in the twelve years which were all that followed the writing of *Queen Mab*, the progress is all in the direction of depth and maturity. I have already paid my tribute to the philosophical merit of the *Defence;* other prose works are fragmentary, but none is despicable. Even the Irish tracts, which are not often referred to, are good polemical writing; the speculations on metaphysics and on morals, and the "Essay on Christianity," are not to be considered as anything but random and interrupted efforts, but they are acute and at times even eloquent. But the best of his philosophy is contained, of course, in his great poems, particularly in *Prometheus Unbound, Epipsychidion* and *Adonais*. In these, abstract thought finds such sensuous and harmonious expression as only Wordsworth rarely rivals, and only Dante frequently excels; there

Language is a perpetual Orphic song,
Which rules with Dædal harmony a throng
Of thoughts and forms, which else senseless and
shapeless were.

66

The particular poetic quality which results from this perfect fusion of thought and feeling we will examine presently; for the moment I am only concerned to defend these poems as the expression of a coherent philosophy or "view of life."   That philosophy Shelley embodied in the myth of Prometheus—the hero of humanity struggling against the tyranny of ignorance and superstition.   Demogorgon's final benediction is too well known to quote, and even hostile critics submit to its supreme poetic power. But the eminence of those verses should not distract us from the more central exposition—Prometheus's speeches towards the end of Act I, for example, and Asia's cosmic vision in Act II, Scene iv, which I will quote:

There was the Heaven and Earth at first,
And Light and Love; then Saturn, from whose throne
Time fell, an envious shadow: such the state
Of the earth's primal spirits beneath his sway,
As the calm joy of flowers and living leaves
Before the wind or sun has withered them
And semivital worms; but he refused
The birthright of their being, knowledge, power,
The skill which wields the elements, the thought
Which pierces this dim universe like light,
Self-empire, and the majesty of love;
For thirst of which they fainted.   Then Prometheus
Gave wisdom, which is strength, to Jupiter,
And with this law alone, 'Let man be free,'
Clothed him with the dominion of wide Heaven.
To know nor faith, nor love, nor law; to be

Omnipotent but friendless is to reign;
And Jove now reigned; for on the race of man
First famine, and then toil, and then disease,
Strife, wounds, and ghastly death unseen before,
Fell; and the unseasonable seasons drove
With alternating shafts of frost and fire,
Their shelterless, pale tribes to mountain caves:
And in their desert hearts fierce wants he sent,
And mad disquietudes, and shadows idle
Of unreal good, which levied mutual war,
So ruining the lair wherein they raged.
Prometheus saw, and waked the legioned hopes
Which sleep within folded Elysian flowers,
Nepenthe, Moly, Amaranth, fadeless blooms,
That they might hide with thin and rainbow wings
The shape of Death; and Love he sent to bind
The disunited tendrils of that vine
Which bears the wine of life, the human heart;
And he tamed fire which, like some beast of prey,
Most terrible, but lovely, played beneath
The frown of man; and tortured to his will
Iron and gold, the slaves and signs of power,
And gems and poisons, and all subtlest forms
Hidden beneath the mountains and the waves.
He gave man speech, and speech created thought,
Which is the measure of the universe;
And Science struck the thrones of earth and heaven,
Which shook, but fell not; and the harmonious mind
Poured itself forth in all-prophetic song;
And music lifted up the listening spirit
Until it walked, exempt from mortal care,

Godlike, o'er the clear billows of sweet sound;
And human first mimicked and then mocked,
With moulded limbs more lovely than its own,
The human form, till marble grew divine;
And mothers, gazing, drank the love men see
Reflected in their race, behold, and perish.
He told the hidden power of herbs and springs,
And Disease drank and slept. Death grew like sleep.
He taught the implicated orbits woven
Of the wide-wandering stars; and how the sun
Changes his lair, and by what secret spell
The pale moon is transformed, when her broad eye
Gazes not on the interlunar sea:
He taught to rule, as life directs the limbs,
The tempest-wingèd chariots of the Ocean,
And the Celt knew the Indian. Cities then
Were built, and through their snow-like columns flowed
The warm winds, and the azure ether shone,
And the blue sea and shadowy hills were seen.
Such, the alleviations of his state,
Prometheus gave to man, for which he hangs
Withering in destined pain. . . .

This is the broadcloth of Shelley's verse, and better to be appreciated in the piece than in the pattern. Against its even goodness the songs and lyrics throw out their lustre. Shelley called this poem a lyrical drama; but actually it is an epic, the greatest expression ever given to humanity's desire for intellectual light and spiritual liberty. The hundred years since it was written is but a very short time in the history of that long effort, and the day may yet come when this poem will take its commanding place in a literature of freedom of which we have yet no conception.

I must not, however, end this section of my argument on a vague exultant note. The riposte must reach its mark. "We may be permitted to infer," Mr. Eliot says, "in so far as the distaste of a person like myself for Shelley's poetry is not attributable to irrelevant prejudices or to a simple blind spot, but is due to a peculiarity in the poetry and not in the reader, that it is not the presentation of beliefs which I do not hold, or—to put the case as extremely as possible—of beliefs which excite my abhorrence, that makes the difficulty. Still less is it that Shelley is deliberately making use of his poetic gifts to propagate a doctrine; for Dante and Lucretius did the same thing. I suggest that the position is somewhat as follows." And then follows the charge of incoherence, immaturity, childishness, feebleness and shabbiness. But we cannot accept the suggestion (and it is only a suggestion: there is no demonstration). On the contrary, we affirm that Shelley's ideas were no more shabby and incoherent than those of Plato who was their chief inspiration; and that in so far as they were unplatonic, they showed a close parallel to the ideas of Lucretius, whom Mr. Eliot accepts. Retracing the steps of his inference, we must come to the conclusion that Mr. Eliot's objection to Shelley's poetry is irrelevant prejudice (for "a simple blind spot" would not excite abhorrence); and such, I would suggest, is the kind of poetic approach of all who believe, with Mr. Eliot, that "literary criticism should be completed by criticism from a definite ethical and theological standpoint."* I do not deny that such criticism may have its interest; but the only kind of criticism which is basic, and therefore complementary not only to literary but also to ethical, theological and every other kind of ideological criticism, is ontogenetic criticism, by which I mean criticism which traces the origins of the work of art in the psychology of the individual and in the economic structure of society.

VI

Shelley's central doctrine—I mean his doctrine of art and morality—is one of more than abstract philosophical interest; it is bound up with the texture of his poetry and the conduct of his life. The principle is simply one of identification; there is no question of the moral value of poetry because poetry and morality proceed from the same source. "The functions of the poetical faculty are twofold; by one it creates new materials of knowledge and power and pleasure; by the other it engenders in the mind a desire to reproduce and arrange them according to a certain rhythm and order which may be called the beautiful and the good." As thus stated, the identity might seem to be merely one of hedonist and æsthetic

* "Religion and Literature," by T. S. Eliot. An essay contributed to *Faith that Illuminates,* edited by V. A. Demant, London, 1935.

values; but Shelley's real meaning is much profounder. The following passage from *A Defence of Poetry* is a famous one, much quoted, but it should be re-read in the present context:

"Ethical science arranges the elements which poetry has created, and propounds schemes and proposes examples of civil and domestic life: nor is it for want of admirable doctrines that men hate, and despise, and censure, and deceive, and subjugate one another. But poetry acts in another and diviner manner. It awakens and enlarges the mind itself by rendering it the receptacle of a thousand unapprehended combinations of thought. Poetry lifts the veil from the hidden beauty of the world, and makes familiar objects be as if they were not familiar; it reproduces all that it represents, and the impersonations clothed in its Elysian light stand thenceforward in the minds of those who have once contemplated them, as memorials of that gentle and exalted content which extends itself over all thoughts and actions with which it coexists. The great secret of morals is love; or a going out of our own nature, and an identification of ourselves with the beautiful which exists in thought, action, or persons, not our own. A man, to be greatly good, must imagine intensely and comprehensively; he must put himself in the place of another and of many others; the pains and pleasures of his species must become his own. The great instrument of moral good is the imagination;

and poetry administers to the effect by acting upon the cause."

We should note, in the first place, how closely this doctrine can be related to the modern psychological doctrine already imparted. "Abstract truths are the personal relics of genius; their vindication in the concrete text of experience is the heritage of our common consciousness. . . . The source of genius is nuclear, original, essential. Moving amid the surface crusts of 'types' which in their restriction of outer contact may only absorb or reflect the impressions about them, genius eradiates from the common centre of our societal organism sustained by an impulse that is cosmic. For this reason, it is the unalterable sentence of genius that it break with every accustomed adherence. It is its law that it raise itself out of habitual inertias and see straight and clear beyond all temporary immediacies, into the unfurbished truth of things." When Dr. Burrow writes like this, he is merely repeating, in very different language, the truth which Shelley expressed with a more direct poetic intuition.

Expressed in these general terms, the moral aspect of Shelley's doctrine might seem harmless enough; "the great secret of morals is love"—that is a sentiment we should all be willing to affirm. But Shelley was one of those uncomfortable idealists who practise what they preach, and it is precisely the practical results of this doctrine from which the timid or the formal moralist recoils in horror or disdain. "Bête!"

"sale!" cries Matthew Arnold. "Blackguard!" cries Mr. Eliot. It is true that there was in his own day another voice that cried: "You were all brutally mistaken about Shelley, who was, without exception, the *best* and least selfish man I ever knew. I never knew one who was not a beast in comparison."* But that was the voice of one who, though he had been stretched on the rack of experience till he touched the extremes of iniquity and glory, and so should speak with profound authority, is admittedly not apt to quell a doctrinaire. There have been others who have forgiven Shelley out of their Christian sympathy, and a few who have dared to imply that a poet of such divine genius is above human laws. But none has attempted to justify Shelley in reason, and on the basis of psychological truth. That, however, is a task which may be attempted with the aid of those psychological considerations which I have brought forward.

The crux of the question is, of course, Shelley's treatment of his first wife, Harriet. If Shelley had not so defiantly deserted her, if he had not so defiantly committed adultery with Mary Godwin, if the consequences of his action had not been so tragic, we should not have had so much righteous indignation about his character and conduct. Shelley's morals would have been confined to a polite essay and to his poetry, and we should have been free to admire the man and his work without distraction. But Shelley sinned against the most

*Byron, in a letter to John Murray, August 3, 1822.

74

sacred clause in the social code of his time, and as a result has been vilified as a person and depreciated as a poet.

Until a few years ago, such judgments were made on a very incomplete knowledge of the facts. It was not until Dr. Leslie Hotson discovered and published Shelley's letters to Harriet written at the time of his parting from her that the full evidence was made available. Dr. Hotson has marshalled that evidence, and presented it with a scholarly detachment from which emerges, on the facts simply, and all idealistic justification apart, a far more favourable view of Shelley's conduct than any that has hitherto prevailed.* The discovery attracted significantly little attention at the time, and now the world is prepared to relapse into its former superficial judgment, which has the sanction of all those forces, those "habitual inertias," which maintain the social code in its hard complacency and fathomless hypocrisy.

I shall not recount the whole story again. A blunt statement of the true circumstances would read somewhat as follows: In the year 1811, a harpy named Eliza Westbrook vamped a youth of nineteen into marrying her sister, a schoolgirl of sixteen. The youth had just been expelled from Oxford for "atheism," was homeless, excited and impressionable, and was moreover the heir to a great estate. The schoolgirl was pretty, neat and witty, but completely under the control of the sister. There was a story of "tyranny"

*Shelley's Lost Letters to Harriet. Edited with an Introduction by Leslie Hotson. (London: Faber & Faber, 1930.)

at home and school, and a threat of suicide if not rescued. The youth, impetuous and romantic, proposed elopement; was eagerly accepted; and the harpy triumphed, even to the extent of fastening herself to the poor deluded couple.* The rest of the story is best told in a few excerpts from the letters of this youth, Shelley:

"1811 (*no date*). What have I said? I declare, quite *ludicrous*. I advised her to resist. She wrote to say that resistance was useless, but that she would fly with me and threw herself upon my protection. We shall have £200 a year; when we find it run short, we must live, I suppose, upon love! Gratitude and admiration, all demand that I should love her *for ever*. (*To Hogg.*)

"*March* 16, 1814. My friend, you are happier than I. You have the pleasures as well as the pains of sensibility. I have sunk into a premature old age of exhaustion, which renders me dead to everything, but the unenviable capacity of indulging the vanity of hope, and a terrible susceptibility to objects of disgust and hatred. (*To Hogg.*)

"(*The same*). Eliza is still with us. . . . I certainly hate her with all my heart and soul. It is a sight which awakens an inexpressible sensation of disgust and horror, to see her caress my poor little

Cf. Hogg: "Harriet Westbrook appears to have been dissatisfied with her school, but without any adequate cause, for she was kindly treated and well educated there. It is not impossible that this discontent was prompted and suggested to her, and that she was put up to it, and to much besides, by somebody, who conducted the whole affair—who had assumed and steadily persisted in keeping the complete direction of her." (Chap. XII.)

76

Ianthe, in whom I may hereafter find the consolation of sympathy. I sometimes feel faint with
the fatigue of checking the overflowings of my
unbounded abhorrence for this miserable wretch.
She is no more than a blind and loathsome worm,
that cannot see to sting. (*To Hogg.*)

"*July,* 1814 (*no date*). I repeat (and believe me,
for I am sincere) that my attachment to you is
unimpaired. I conceive that it has acquired even
a deeper and more lasting character, that it is now
less exposed than ever to the fluctuations of
phantasy or caprice. Our connection was not one
of passion and impulse. Friendship was its basis,
and on this basis it has enlarged and strengthened.
It is no reproach to me that you have never filled
my heart with an all-sufficing passion; perhaps you
are even yourself a stranger to these impulses,
which one day may be awakened by some nobler
and worthier than me; and you may find a lover
as passionate and faithful, as I shall ever be a
friend affectionate and sincere! (*To Harriet.*)

"*September* 15, 1814. You think that I have injured
you. Since I first beheld you almost, my chief
study has been to overwhelm you with benefits.
Even now when a violent and lasting passion for
another leads me to prefer her society to yours, I
am perpetually employed in devising how I can
be permanently and truly useful to you, in what
manner my time and my fortune may be most
securely expended for your real interests. In return
for this it is not well that I should be wounded with

reproach and blame: so unexampled and singular an attachment demands a return far different. And it would be generous, nay even just, to consider with kindness that woman whom my judgment and my heart have selected as the noblest and the most excellent of human beings. (*To Harriet.*)

"*September* 27, 1814. A common love for all that the world detests was once the bond of union between us. This you have been the first to break; and you have lost a friend whom you will with difficulty replace. Your contumelious language toward Mary is equally impotent and mean. You appeal to the vilest superstitions of the most ignorant and slavish of mankind. I consider it an insult that you address such cant to me. (*To Harriet.*)

"*? October* 3, 1814. I am united to another; you are no longer my wife. Perhaps I have done you injury, but surely most innocently and unintentionally, in having commenced any connexion with you. That injury, whatever be its amount, was not to be avoided. (*To Harriet.*)"

Such excerpts do not convey the whole story, but the full letters are there for any reader to consult. They must be supplemented by some estimate of the personality of Harriet, such as I have attempted for the personality of Shelley. But whatever conclusion we reached on the basis of the somewhat contradictory evidence, it would not affect the issue. Harriet may have been an angel in the house, with all the virtues of a good wife and an intelligent companion; or she may have been an extremely frivolous and tiresome schoolgirl, with a mania for self-destruction, incapable of passion as of understanding. In either case, she and Shelley were victims of life's most cruel joke (life, in this instance, being to a considerable extent personified in Eliza). Shelley, in his dilemma, might have kept the code and earned the approval of future moralists; but we do not know to what alternative tragedy he and Harriet would have drifted. Out of the fullness of his heart and the strength of his philosophy he elected his individual liberty. He earned immediate opprobrium and more than a century of calumny; but he lifted himself out of a premature old age of exhaustion, into a brighter element of intellectual vitality, and into a new lease of poetic inspiration.

Earlier in his life, shortly before he was married to Harriet Westbrook, Shelley had upheld against Hogg the proposition that "laws were not made for men of honour." He then argued the case, as eloquently as any undergraduate, with appeals to Aristotle and Godwin. Three years later he had to argue the case in his own destiny, and deep within his own being he found that philosophy of love which is the theme of his greatest poetry. A superficial and a cynical mind will only see in such philosophical poetry a rationalisation of Shelley's selfish instincts; but from our nearer and more sympathetic point of view we can have a deeper appreciation of a feeling too organic to be selfish, too magnanimous to be immoral, and too hopeful, in "this cold common hell, our life," to be denied.

VII

The particular quality of Shelley's poetry still remains to be defined. It is a quality directly related to the nature of his personality, and that is why I have taken so much trouble to describe that personality. Understanding the personality, we may more easily, more openly, appreciate the poetry.

Byron, who was a very honest critic, even of his friends, was the first to be aware of Shelley's *particular* quality. "You know my high opinion of your own poetry," he wrote to Shelley, and added the reason: "—because it is of *no* school." To Byron all the rest of his contemporaries seemed "second-hand" imitators of antique models or doctrinaire exponents of a mannerism. Shelley alone could not be so simply classified; his verse was too honestly original, too independently thought and wrought, to be accepted as "fashionable literature." For there are always these two types of originality: originality that responds like the Æolian harp to every gust of contemporary feeling, pleasing by its anticipation of what is but half-formed in the public consciousness; and originality that is not influenced by anything outside the poet's own consciousness, but is the direct product of his individual mind and independent feeling. The latter type is always long in winning recognition, and since Shelley's originality was essentially of this type, we need not be surprised that only a few of his contemporaries appreciated his poetry for its proper qualities.

The reaction of Keats is the most interesting, for he had perhaps a profounder understanding of the nature of poetry than any man of that age—profounder, I would say, than Byron and even profounder than Coleridge. We only discern this from the occasional statements made in his letters—there is unfortunately no formal essay to compare with Shelley's. Nor did Keats live to write poetry with which he was personally satisfied; we must not, that is to say, treat the poetry of Keats as an exemplification of his poetic ideals. A detailed comparison of the poetry of Keats and Shelley would not therefore be of great value. But Keats's reaction to Shelley's poetry, expressed in a letter to Shelley, is most definitely critical:

" . . . You might curb your magnanimity and be more of an artist, and load every rift of your subject with ore. The thought of such discipline must fall like cold chains upon you, who perhaps never sat with your wings furled for six months together."

We cannot doubt the force of the impact which Shelley's poetry had made on Keats. The poetry had been felt, but felt as something strange or inadequate. And actually we can see that what is involved is a clash of personalities. There is no need to describe Keats's personality at length; but it was in no way parallel to Shelley's. Keats was not, of course, a normal type—no genius is; but compared with Shelley he was far more fully adjusted to his environment; physically more masculine and heterosexual; and though a sick man ("when I shook him by the hand there was death"), not a morbid one. Sensitive critics have even been considerably disturbed by what they regard as a deplorable strain of coarseness and vulgarity in his nature. Without going into any great detail, it will be obvious that the general mode of expression of such a personality would be very different from Shelley's; it would, by a process contrary to the one we have described in Shelley's case, show a tendency towards definiteness and objectivity. Now though much of Keats's poetry is anything but definite and objective, he was very conscious of an intolerable hiatus between his personality and the poetic diction he had derived from traditional models and current fashions; and his whole effort, as expressed in his short but intense poetic development, is towards objective virtues.

The whole tendency of Shelley, on the contrary, is towards a clarification and abstraction of thought—away from the personal and the particular towards the general and the universal. Between the transcendental intellectualism of Shelley and the concrete sensualism of Keats there could be, and was no contact.

The highest beauties of Keats's poetry are enumerative: a positive evocation of the tone and texture of physical objects. Even when describing an abstract conception like Melancholy, the imagery of physical sensation is dominant:

Ay, in the very temple of Delight
  Veil'd Melancholy has her sovran shrine,
    Though seen of none save him whose strenuous tongue
Can burst Joy's grape against his palate fine . . .

But the highest beauties of Shelley's poetry are evanescent and imponderable—thought so tenuous and intuitive, that it has no visual equivalent; no positive impact:

Life of Life! thy lips enkindle
  With their love the breath between them;
And thy smiles before they dwindle
  Make the cold air fire; then screen them
In those looks, where whoso gazes
Faints, entangled in their mazes.

Child of Light! thy limbs are burning
  Through the vest which seems to hide them;
As the radiant lines of morning
  Through the clouds ere they divide them;
And this atmosphere divinest
Shrouds thee whereso'er thou shinest.

Fair are others; none beholds thee,
  But thy voice sounds low and tender
Like the fairest, for it folds thee
  From the sight, that liquid splendour,
And all feel, yet see thee never,
As I feel now, lost for ever!

Lamp of Earth! where'er thou movest
  Its dim shapes are clad with brightness,
And the souls of whom thou lovest
  Walk upon the winds with lightness,
Till they fail, as I am failing,
Dizzy, lost, yet unbewailing!

In such a poem—and it is the supreme type of Shelley's poetic utterance—every image fades into air, every outline is dissolved in fire. The idea conveyed—the notional content—is almost negligible; the poetry exists in the suspension of meaning, in the avoidance of actuality.

In other words, such poetry has no precision, and the process of its unfolding is not logical. It does not answer to a general definition of any kind. It is vain to apply to it that method of criticism which assumes that the ardour of a verse can be analysed into separate vocables, and that poetry is a function of sound. Poetry is mainly a function of language— the exploitation of a medium, a vocal and mental material, in the interests of a personal mood or emotion, or of the thoughts evoked by such moods and emotions. I do not think we can say much more about it; according to our sensitivity we recognise its success. The rest of our reasoning about it is either mere prejudice, ethical anxiety, or academic pride.

Among his contemporaries, Shelley was perhaps nearest in poetic quality to Landor, whose *Gebir* was a lasting joy to him. A critical justification for this attraction would not be far to seek. The next nearest analogies are with Schiller and Goethe, both of whom Shelley read with enthusiasm; the influence of *Faust* has been traced in *The Triumph of Life*,* but between Goethe and Shelley there is a general sympathy of poetic outlook which is not explained by direct contacts. Other analogies, some of which I have already mentioned, are remoter: "the gentle seriousness, the delicate sensibility, the calm and sustained energy" of Ariosto; and above all "the first awakener of entranced Europe . . . the congregator of those great spirits who presided over the resurrection of learning; the Lucifer of that starry flock which in the thirteenth century shone forth from republican Italy as from a heaven, into the darkness of the benighted world"—Dante. All great poetry, said Shelley in the same reference to Dante, is *infinite;* and that is the final quality of his own poetry, the quality which lifts it into regions beyond the detractions of moralists and sciolists.

Shelley is of no school; that is to say, Shelley is above all schools, universal in the mode of his expression and the passion of his mind. That passion, the force that urged him to abundant voice, was simple, almost single, in its aim. "I knew Shelley more intimately than any man," wrote Hogg, "but I never could discern in him any more than two fixed principles. The first was a strong, irrepressible love of liberty; of liberty in the abstract, and somewhat after the pattern of the ancient

* F. Melian Stawell, "Shelley's *Triumph of Life*," English Association: *Essays and Studies*, Vol. V, p. 105.

republics, without reference to the English constitution, respecting which he knew little and cared nothing, heeding it not at all. The second was an equally ardent love of toleration of all opinions, but more especially of religious opinions; of toleration, complete, entire, universal, unlimited; and, as a deduction and corollary from which latter principle, he felt an intense abhorrence of persecution of every kind, public or private." Liberty and toleration—these words have a tortured history, and are often perverted for a moral purpose. But that was not Shelley's intention. "The highest moral purpose aimed at in the highest species of the drama, is the teaching the human heart, through its sympathies and antipathies, the knowledge of itself; in proportion to the possession of which knowledge, every human being is wise, just, sincere, tolerant and kind." Inasmuch as the final quality of Shelley's poetry is infinitude, so the final quality of his mind is sympathy. Sympathy and infinitude—these are expansive virtues, not avowed in the dry air of disillusion, awaiting a world of peace and justice for their due recognition.

COVENTRY PATMORE

COVENTRY PATMORE was recently described as "the most neglected of our notable poets";* even his grave, we were told, is untended, and fit to illustrate one of his best lines:

"The darnell'd garden of unheedful death."

And this would seem to be all the comment which time has made on the proud words which Patmore placed in front of the collected edition of his poems:

"I have respected posterity; and, should there be a posterity which cares for letters, I dare to hope it will respect me."

Perhaps we have not lived long enough to earn the name of posterity; perhaps we do not care sufficiently for letters to honour the grave of a poet who made no compromise with the public of his own day, and can therefore expect none from the public of ours. But that is not the real truth. Whenever a critic of faithful conscience recalls the poets of this period— Tennyson, Arnold, Clough, Patmore, Browning, Rossetti—it is on the name of Patmore that he lingers with a still lively sense of wonder. The rest have been fully estimated, and their influence, if not exhausted, is predictable. Patmore is still potential; but to what extent, and whether purely as a poet or more likely as a mystic, are questions which must be

*By Mr. Clifford Bax in a letter to *The Times Literary Supplement*, May 12, 1932.

answered in this essay.

That arrogance which dominates all contemporary accounts of Patmore's personality is the first quality we must dwell on, because it is a reflex of the man's relation to his age. No poet, indeed, no personality of the whole period stands in such direct opposition to all its beliefs and ideals—perhaps we should say, finally stood in such opposition, for Patmore's settled attitude did not develop until middle age. He began his career with family circumstances which explain a good deal—a harsh unsympathetic mother, and a father, who though sympathetic to the extent of spoiling him in every direction—particularly in the direction of a literary career—was regarded by the world at large as a cad and impostor, till he finally fled the country to escape his financial entanglements. Such circumstances are bound to produce in a sensitive nature "defence" compensations which take on the appearance of self-assertion and intellectual arrogance. And these are perhaps the very factors which, whilst they explain the "drive" of a personality like Patmore's, also give us a clue to its creative limitations.

Patmore once declared that he was the only poet of his generation, except Barnes, who steadily maintained a literary conscience. This is perfectly true. He was a *clerc* who never betrayed that tradition of intellectual integrity of which every poet should be the trustee. Everything he wrote was written with a great sense of responsibility, not only to the public, but to his own inner light or inspiration. Though his first considerable work, *The Angel in the House*, won an immense popularity, he deliberately turned his back on this success, to pursue a path implicit in his faith which led him to intellectual heights where no considerable public could then follow, and which will always be reserved for the select. In politics he was bitterly opposed to all parties. Gladstone he abhorred so thoroughly that he could write of him:

His leprosy's so perfect men call him clean;

and his scorn of Disraeli and "the false English Nobles" was equally vitriolic. In contrast to the prevailing economic and political optimism, he adopted views of unrelieved pessimism. He saw himself (alone with Barnes!) as the last classical author of a civilisation on the verge of extinction:

"Unpalatable and unacceptable as the suggestion may be, it cannot be denied by persons who are able and willing to look facts in the face that there are already strong indications of a relapse into a long-protracted period of social and political disorganisation, so complete that there shall be no means of leisure or even living for a learned class, nor any audience for what it has to impart. Such recrudescences of civilisation have occurred, and they may occur again, though the prospect may be as incredible to most Europeans at the present moment as it must have been to the lieges of the Eternal City at the height and sudden turning-point of its popular glory and seemingly con-solidated order."

In religion he became, again in opposition to the intellectual trend of his period, a Catholic of the most intransigent type; and even in his religion he was so little in sympathy with its temporal vessels that he continually murmured against the priesthood and even against the Pope.

This attitude was maintained with a courage and absence of reserve which we cannot but admire. "Plain-speaking," he says in one of his essays, "does not vitiate. Even coarseness is health compared with those suppressed forms of the disease of impurity which come of our modern undivine silences." And it was one of his first principles that there existed an absolute incompatibility between genius and any kind of insincerity. This belief is stated with great force in an essay in *Religio Poetæ*, the purpose of which is to distinguish the intellect from the understanding (or discursive reason) and the memory as the peculiar faculty of genius:

> "The intellect is the faculty of the 'seer.' It discerns truth as a living thing; and, according as it is in less or greater power, it discerns with a more or less far-seeing glance the relationships of principles to each other, and of facts, circumstances, and the realities of nature to principles, without anything that can be properly called ratiocination. It cannot be cultivated, as the understanding and memory can be and need to be; and it cannot in the ordinary course of things be injured, except by one means—namely, dishonesty, that is, habitual denial

by the will, for the sake of interested or vicious
motives, of its own perceptions. Genius and high
moral—not necessarily physical—courage are therefore found to be constant companions. Indeed, it is
difficult to say how far an absolute moral courage
in acknowledging intuitions may not be of the very
nature of genius: and whether it might not be
described as a sort of interior sanctity which dares
to see and confess to itself that it sees, though its
vision should place it in a minority of one."

This courage Patmore himself possessed in the
highest degree, and certainly he did not shrink from
finding himself in a minority of one. Admitting this,
it only remains for us to consider critically the
quality of his vision and his ability to body it forth.

Perhaps we might consider the more technical
question first. By this I mean Patmore's whole
conception of poetry as an art, and then his own
particular style. Both aspects of the question give rise
to the most searching doubts. The problem is
simplified for us by the compactness and cohesion of
Patmore's verse. It can without loss be reduced to
two parts—to two sequences of poems distinct in style
if not in matter. *The Angel in the House* was one of the
most characteristic and certainly one of the most
successful poems of the whole Victorian age: it had
sold over a quarter of a million copies before the
author's death. The first part was originally published in 1854; the final part in 1863. It belongs to
that bastard type of literature—the novel in verse—

and has much of the atmosphere and, for those who like it, the charm of the domestic fiction of the period. It was fairly characterised by Edmund Gosse as "humdrum stories of girls that smell of bread and butter," but it cannot be dismissed at that. Of its philosophy I shall have something to say presently; meanwhile its subject-matter raises a question of importance which has never been squarely faced by Patmore's apologists. If necessary we might go back to Aristotle for reasons, but surely it may be laid down as self-evident that poetry and life are anything but identical. The sphere of poetry is at once rarer and more remote than the sphere of life, a truth which will only imply a separation of art and life to those who confuse life with existence. Art involves æsthetic distance. Contemporary subjects can only be treated if invested with dignity or obscurity—and Patmore's "girls" have neither. The theme which Patmore proposed to himself was right enough. "The Siren woman," he claimed, "had been often sung by the Pagan Poets of all time, and the Fairy woman by the Troubadours of the Middle Ages. But that Love in which all Loves centre, and that Woman who is the rightful sustainer of them all, the Inspiration of Youth, and the Consolation of Age, that Love and that Woman had seldom been sung sincerely and effectually." That is true enough, but such love need not necessarily be pictured in the decorous and depressing atmosphere of a Victorian Deanery. It is significant that the original of the Dean was in real life a Nonconformist minister, but even Patmore saw that he could not make poetry out of nonconformity: it was his mistake to imagine that the snobbish atmosphere of a Cathedral Close would make all the difference. When it was too late Patmore realised his mistake, and he spent the last phase of his life dreaming of, and preparing for, a great poem on the Marriage of the Virgin, in which the same love was to be celebrated, but with distance and circumstance worthy of the theme.

This defect of presentation explains why *The Angel* is not read to-day; and I can imagine no posterity which will reverse our present inclination in this matter. It has become and will remain a literary curiosity, not justified by any remarkable beauties even of texture or expression. For it has to be admitted, next, that Patmore at this stage of his inspiration was no inevitable poet. He chose a simple metre for his simple subject—iambic octo-syllabic—and laboured hard to make it smooth. But as Tennyson said, some of his lines seemed "hammered up out of old nails," and though such lines were pointed out to him, he was often incapable of seeing anything wrong with them, and there are plenty left in the final version. That would not matter so much if there were corresponding jewels of highest light, to outshine these defects, but actually the texture is sustained at an even level of apt but uninspired expression. It is wit-writing of an extremely competent and felicitous kind, but is not, and perhaps never pretended to be, lyrical poetry of any emotional intensity.

This is the more remarkable because no poet since Wordsworth and Coleridge, not even Matthew Arnold, had such a clear conception of the poet's function. In that essay, extremely compressed with sense, which gives the title to the volume *Religio Poetæ*, we find the best expression of Patmore's views. The Poet is compared with the Saint: he is above all the *perceiver*, "nothing having any interest for him unless he can, as it were, see it and touch it with the spiritual senses, with which he is pre-eminently endowed."

"The Poet, again, is not more singular for the delicacy of his spiritual insight, which enables him to see celestial beauty and substantial reality where all is blank to most others, than for the surprising range and alertness of vision, whereby he detects, in external nature, those likenesses and echoes by which spiritual realities can alone be rendered credible and more or less apparent, or subject to 'real apprehension,' in persons of inferior perceptive powers. Such likenesses, when chosen by the imagination, not the fancy, of the true Poet, are *real* words—the only real words; for 'that which is unseen is known by that which is seen,' and natural similitudes often contain and are truly the visible *ultimates* of the unseen. . . .

"He gives the world to eat only of the Tree of Life, reality; and will not so much as touch the Tree of Knowledge, as the writer of Genesis ironically calls the Tree of Learning that leads to denial of knowledge. He is the very reverse of a 'scientist.' "

This emphasis on the realism of words is in advance of anything suggested by Coleridge. It is to be found in Vico, whom Patmore could hardly have read, but only receives its full development in the present-day theories of Croce and Vivante. It was his firm faith in this theory which reconciled Patmore to the intermittency of his inspiration. When a poet *knows* what poetry is, he cannot be false to his genius. It would be a spiritual betrayal which could only end in spiritual death. Patmore had genius enough to perceive this, and I think that it was this very concentration on the nature of poetry which led him towards the wider mysticism of the Catholic faith. In another essay in *Religio Poetæ* he says:

"The most peculiar and characteristic mark of genius is insight into subjects which are dark to ordinary vision and for which ordinary language has no adequate expression. Imagination is rather the language of genius: the power which traverses at a single glance the whole external universe, and seizes on the likenesses and images, and their combinations, which are best able to embody ideas and feelings otherwise inexpressible; so that the 'things which are unseen are known by the things which are seen.' "

And elsewhere he says: "Sensible things alone can be expressed fully and directly by sensible terms.

97

Symbols and parable, and metaphors—which are parables on a small scale—are the only means of adequately conveying, or rather hinting, supersensual knowledge." Patmore's own poetry, in its final and most important phase, was to become just such a hinting at supersensual knowledge. But this change of spirit was dependent on a change of form.

Patmore's poetic technique received an immense impetus from his invention of what was virtually a new verse-form—the "ode" which he began to use about 1865. A certain degree of originality in formal structure has perhaps been a condition of all exceptional poetry—novelty of means acting as a spur to any kind of individual attainment. Edmund Gosse was of the opinion that Patmore found the analogy for his "ode" in the *Canzoniere* of Petrarch. Patmore himself tried to find sanction for his form in the historical development of the ode in English poetry, but these pedantic notions of his are not very convincing. The form, in fact, developed under the stress of a particular mode of feeling. To quote a comparatively simple example:

A FAREWELL

With all my will, but much against my heart,
We two now part.
My Very Dear,
Our solace is, the sad road lies so clear.
It needs no art,

98

With faint, averted feet
And many a tear,
In our opposed paths to persevere.
Go thou to East, I West.
We will not say
There's any hope, it is so far away.
But, O, my Best,
When the one darling of our widowhead,
The nursling Grief,
Is dead,
And no dews blur our eyes
To see the peach-bloom come in evening skies,
Perchance we may,
Where now this night is day,
And even through faith of still averted feet,
Making full circle of our banishment,
Amazed meet;
The bitter journey to the bourne so sweet
Seasoning the termless feast of our content
With tears of recognition never dry.

It will be seen that the Patmorean ode is, in short, an iambic measure (like that of *The Angel in the House*), which, however, breaks away from the regularity of the octosyllabic couplet or quatrain to indulge in what Patmore himself called "the fine irregular rock of the free tetrameter." The verse in these Odes moves "in long undulating strains" which are modulated by pauses and irregularly occurring rhymes, the rhymed words determining the length of the lines which vary arbitrarily from two to ten or even twelve syllables. It is therefore a metre of extraordinary freedom and impetuous force—which only needed the internal freedom introduced by Patmore's friend Hopkins to give us all the constituents of modern free verse. "The beauty and incomparable variety of the metre," wrote Patmore in a letter published in Mr. Champneys' *Memoirs*, "opens up quite a new prospect to me of the possibilities of poetry"; and again: "I have hit upon *the* finest metre that ever was invented, and on *the* finest mine of wholly unworked material that ever fell to the lot of an English poet." It is interesting to note that some years after he had invented this measure, Patmore entered into a long correspondence with the poet mentioned above, whose technical innovations were to become the greatest source of inspiration to our own generation. Gerard Manley Hopkins's letters to Patmore are said to be "numerous, long and of great interest," and "so excellent, so full of the writer's individuality, of acute if sometimes whimsical judgments, that they are all worthy of preservation"; but Mr. Champneys refrains from publishing them as being too technical for the general reader. It is good to know that these letters have been preserved, and will one day be given to the world; for we dip here into the living stream of English poetical development, and Hopkins's reactions to Patmore's technique should be of the greatest interest. The correspondence might prove that Hopkins was, in some degree, influenced by Patmore; and Hopkins undoubtedly induced Patmore to make many revisions in his poems.

The Odes, begun about 1865, represent Patmore's output for the rest of his life—about thirty years; and yet they only occupy a hundred pages in the collected edition of his works. This comparative paucity may be explained by the high standard of literary morality which Patmore set himself. "Every one of my books," he wrote, "has been written after many years of reflection on its subject—reflection for my own benefit, not primarily with a view to the book, and has been merely the easy and rapid overflowing into words of the fullness of thought at last attained." And as a corollary to this we find him saying: "My best things were written most quickly. 'Amelia' took four days; 'Deliciæ Sapientiæ de Amore' two hours; several of the best Odes even less." Perhaps it was a mistake thus to wait for thought voluntarily to move harmonious numbers—perhaps it is always a mistake to conceive poetry as a species of divine visitation—Hopkins was of that opinion. But Patmore made this attendance on inspiration almost an article of religious faith, and though he worked in preparation for a poem with solemn deliberation, he never once forced his muse to unwilling expression.

Possibly an explanation of the intermittency of his inspiration is to be found in the nature of Patmore's personality. He himself was fond of making a distinction between the masculine and the feminine mind in literature. For instance, in his essay on "Mrs. Meynell," he says: "A strong and predominatingly masculine mind has often much to say, but a very imperfect ability to say it; the predominatingly feminine mind can say anything, but has nothing to say; but with the double-sexed insight of genius, realities and expressions are wedded from their first conceptions, and, even in their least imposing development are living powers, and of more practical importance than the results of the highest efforts of mind when either of its factors greatly predominates over the other." He found Mrs. Meynell too deficient in this "*ultimate* womanhood, the expressional *body*," to give her a right to be counted among the classical poets. The same charge might, I think, be made against Patmore himself. Edmund Gosse* records that "during the debateable period between his first wife's death and his second marriage, Patmore's ideas with regard to poetry underwent a very remarkable change. In later life he was accustomed to insist on the essential oneness of his work, and to point to its uniform features. But setting his eloquent casuistry aside, the reader cannot fail to see a very broad chasm lying between what he wrote up to 1862, and what he wrote after that date. In the first place the appeal to a popular judgment, to a wide circle of amiable readers, entirely disappears. Patmore, with the removal of so many earthly ties, and with the growth of what was mystical and transcendental in his temperament, became haughty in his attitude to the world. His conscientiousness as an artist was quickened, and at the same time he gave way to a species of intellectual

Coventry Patmore, by Edmund Gosse (1905), pp. 124–5.

arrogance which had always been dormant in his nature, but which now took the upper hand."

This intellectual arrogance represents a certain settling of his fluent feminine personality, the psychological condition of his poetic force, along firm lines of masculine character inhibitive to this force, and there can be little doubt that this tendency was immensely accelerated by the decision he had to make about this time—he had not only to compromise in some degree with his doctrine of the inviolability of nuptial love, but concurrently was impelled by his conscience to make the final act of submission and become a member of the Catholic Church. The complex strands of this psychological development cannot be unravelled here, and I am far from suggesting that this individual case reveals any general rule; but in plain fact Patmore did emerge from this mental turmoil with his masculine arrogance intensified, and with the frequency of his poetic impulse in consequence impaired.

It is time now to consider the substance of Patmore's poetry. Mr. Arthur Symons once described Patmore as "a poet of one idea and of one metre," and it is indeed amazing to see the alacrity with which he first adopted his central idea, and the tenacity with which he developed it and intensified it. Already in the more philosophical parts of *The Angel in the House*—in those Preludes and Devices which interrupt the narrative and in "The Wedding Sermon" with which it concludes—Patmore had outlined his conception of love. Incidentally, these

Preludes often display a complex fusion of fantasy and wit which puts them on the highest level of English metaphysical poetry: I quote "The Amaranth" as an example of this type:

> Feasts satiate; stars distress with height;
>   Friendship means well, but misses reach,
> And wearies in its best delight
>   Vex'd with the vanities of speech;
> Too long regarded, roses even
>   Afflict the mind with fond unrest;
> And to converse direct with Heaven
>   Is oft a labour in the breast;
> Whate'er the up-looking soul admires,
>   Whate'er the senses' banquet be,
> Fatigues at last with vain desires,
>   Or sickens by satiety;
> But truly my delight was more
>   In her to whom I'm bound for aye
> Yesterday than the day before,
>   And more to-day than yesterday.

As for the philosophy which underlies the whole structure of *The Angel*, and which was to be developed into rarer mystical concepts in the Odes, it has never been better summarised than by Patmore himself in an essay on "Love and Poetry" which appears in *Religio Poetæ*.

"The whole of after-life depends very much upon how life's transient transfiguration in youth by love is subsequently regarded; and the greatest of

all the functions of the poet is to aid in his readers
the fulfilment of the cry, which is that of nature as
well as religion, 'Let not my heart forget the things
mine eyes have seen.' The greatest perversion of
the poet's function is to falsify the memory of that
transfiguration of the senses and to make light of its
sacramental character. This character is instantly
recognised by the unvitiated heart and apprehension of every youth and maiden; but it is very
easily forgotten and profaned by most, unless its
sanctity is upheld by priests and poets. Poets are
naturally its prophets—all the more powerful
because, like the prophets of old, they are wholly
independent of the priests, and are often the first to
discover and rebuke the lifelessness into which that
order is always tending to fall. If society is to
survive its apparently impending dangers, it must
be mainly by guarding and increasing the purity of
the sources in which society begins. The world is
finding out, as it has often done before, that it
cannot do without religion. Love is the first thing
to wither under its loss. What love does in transfiguring life, that religion does in transfiguring love:
as any one may see who compares one state or time
with another. Love is sure to be something less than
human if it is not something more; and the so-
called extravagances of the youthful heart, which
always claim a character for divinity in its
emotions, fall necessarily into sordid, if not shameful, reaction, if those claims are not justified to the
understanding by the faith which declares man and

woman to be priest and priestess to each other of relations inherent in Divinity itself, and proclaimed in the words 'Let us make man in our own image' and 'male and female create he them.' "

The mystical developments of this philosophy received a perfect prose expression in that lost masterpiece, the *Sponsa Dei*, which Patmore destroyed when Hopkins warned him that it was "telling secrets," and that he ought to submit it to his spiritual director. Edmund Gosse, who had read the manuscript, says that "no existing specimen of Patmore's prose seems to me so delicate, or penetrated by quite so high a charm of style." And the subject, he says, "was certainly audacious. It was not more or less than an interpretation of the love between the soul and God by an analogy of the love between a woman and a man; it was, indeed, a transcendental treatise on divine desire seen through the veil of human desire. The purity and crystalline passion of the writer carried him safely over the most astounding difficulties."

One cannot help regretting the destruction of this work (as we regret the poems which Hopkins, for similar scruples, himself destroyed), but actually I doubt if much of the substance of Patmore's doctrine has been lost. It is all implicit in the Odes, and in that book of maxims which is one of the greatest of Patmore's achievements: *The Rod, the Root, and the Flower* (an English work which it is not wholly ridiculous to compare with Pascal's *Pensées*). The following Ode "To the Body" may be given as an example of the daring, and the impetuosity (there are only three sentences in it), and the final intensity of Patmore's poetry:

> Creation's and Creator's crowning good;
> Wall of infinitude;
> Foundation of the sky,
> In Heaven forecast
> And long'd for from eternity,
> Though laid the last;
> Reverberating dome,
> Of music cunningly built home
> Against the void and indolent disgrace
> Of unresponsive space;
> Little sequester'd pleasure-house
> For God and for His Spouse;
> Elaborately, yea, past conceiving, fair,
> Since, from the graced decorum of the hair,
> Ev'n to the tingling, sweet
> Soles of the simple, earth-confiding feet,
> And from the inmost heart
> Outwards unto the thin
> Silk curtains of the skin,
> Every least part
> Astonish'd hears
> And sweet replies to some like region of the spheres;
> Form'd for a dignity prophets but darkly name,
> Less shameless men cry "Shame!"
> So rich with wealth conceal'd
> That Heaven and Hell fight chiefly for this field;

Clinging to everything that pleases thee
With indefectible fidelity;
Alas, so true
To all thy friendships that no grace
Thee from thy sin can wholly disembrace;
Which thus 'bides with thee as the Jebusite,
That, maugre all God's promises could do,
The chosen People never conquer'd quite;
Who therefore lived with them,
And that by formal truce and as of right,
In metropolitan Jerusalem.
For which false fealty
Thou needs must, for a season, lie
In the grave's arms, foul and unshriven,
Albeit, in Heaven,
Thy crimson-throbbing Glow
Into its old abode aye pants to go,
And does with envy see
Enoch, Elijah, and the Lady, she
Who left the roses in her body's lieu.
O, if the pleasures I have known in thee
But my poor faith's poor first fruits be,
What quintessential, keen, ethereal bliss
Then shall be his
Who has thy birth-time's consecrating dew
For death's sweet chrism retain'd,
Quick, tender, virginal, and unprofaned!

Even at its best Patmore's poetry is spoilt by ugly inversions and elisions, inexcusable considering the freedom of the form. But in these last Odes, we are hardly aware of such faults: the thought is irredeemably fused in the expression, and the result is true poetry of the rarest and perhaps the highest kind—metaphysical poetry such as Lucretius, Dante, Donne, Crashaw and Wordsworth wrote. Those who limit poetry by a narrow lyrical conception of the art will find little to charm their indolence in Patmore. But those who are braced to the highest levels of the art, where the flowers are few and fugitive, where Nature and Humanity, to adapt a saying of Patmore's, are beautified and developed instead of being withered up by religious thought, will find in the best of the Odes a fund of inspired poetry for which they would willingly sacrifice the whole baggage of the Victorian legacy in general. And they will find this poetry amply supported by Patmore's prose, to which justice is not often done— prose which has "the virile qualities of simplicity, continuity and positiveness."

Of the fundamental faith to which all Patmore's writings are finally related, it would be presumptuous to do more than point out quite dispassionately its vigour, its broad-mindedness, and its essential freedom. It was a faith opposed to the whole trend, literary and scientific, of Patmore's period. Patmore was not afraid to scale his isolated peak, but in this he had the good sense to abate some of his usual arrogance. His last word is given in the Preface to *The Rod, the Root, and the Flower*, written in 1895, the year before his death:

"Far be it from me to pose as other than a mere reporter, using the poetic intellect and imagination so as in part to conceive those happy realities of life which in many have been and are an actual and abiding possession; and to express them in such a manner that thousands who lead beautiful and substantially Catholic lives, whether outside or within the visible Church, may be assisted in the only true learning, which is to know better that which they already know."

GERARD MANLEY HOPKINS

"The fine delight that fathers thought."

I

THE life of Gerard Manley Hopkins, like the lives of most poets, was outwardly monotonous; how can the life of the true poet, who is the direct opposite of the man of action, be otherwise? He was born on the 11th of June, 1844, his father and mother being of cultured middle-class stock. He died at the age of forty-five in 1889. Between these two necessary events, there are only two others which have any vital significance—his conversion to the Catholic Church in 1866, and his ordination to the priesthood in 1877. Nevertheless, a life was never more intensely lived: for he lived acutely with all his senses. He became a poet, but he might have been a musician— all his life, we are told, he was composing songs and melodies; and he might have been a painter—he had great aptitude in drawing and was advised to adopt painting as a profession. Finally, he had another kind of sensibility which is so often overlooked—I mean that sensibility for the quality and contour of ideas, on which the true metaphysician depends. He dreamed his way through childhood—bookish, pallid, desperately strong-willed and courageous; precocious, perhaps not a little pretentious. He wrote long elaborate prize-poems at school, poems too full of learning to have any suggestion of original genius. At Oxford he came under the influence of

Jowett, and was, one of his friends* tells us, "at first a little tinged with the liberalism prevalent among reading men." But only at first. The same friend describes a walking tour he took with Hopkins in 1865, during which they visited the Benedictine monastery at Belmont, near Hereford. There they had a long conversation with Canon Raynal, afterwards Abbot. Hopkins was impressed. His mood gave birth to a poem in which his first genuine note is struck:

> *I have desired to go*
> *Where springs not fail,*
> *To fields where flies no sharp and sided hail*
> *And a few lilies blow.*

> *And I have asked to be*
> *Where no storms come,*
> *Where the green swell is in the havens dumb*
> *And out of the swing of the sea.*

That "Heaven-haven," so complete in its spiritual complacency, was never to be Hopkins's own lot. His faith was to be tense, but not firm; it was to be all the stronger because held in opposition to his obstinate reasonings.

Oxford in the 'sixties was still reckoning with the Tractarian Movement. A youth the innate religious tendencies of Hopkins was inevitably drawn into the discipleship of Dr. Pusey. But

---

*William Addis: quoted in *Gerard Manley Hopkins*, by G. F. Lahey, S.J. (Oxford, 1930), a memoir to which I owe these details of Hopkins's life.

beyond Dr. Pusey was the greater mind, the clearer intelligence, the poetic sensibility of Newman. He rose like a great golden eagle above all the contemporaries of Hopkins, and under his wings Hopkins inevitably sheltered. In 1866 we find him addressing Newman "with great hesitation," but coming straight to the point:

"I am anxious to become a Catholic . . . I do not want to be helped to any conclusions of belief, for I am thankful to say my mind is made up, but the necessity of becoming a Catholic (although I have long foreseen where the only consistent position would lie) coming on me suddenly has put me into painful confusion of mind about my immediate duty in my circumstances. I wished also to know what it would be morally my duty to hold on certain formally open points, because the same reasoning which makes the Tractarian ground contradictory would almost lead one also to shrink from what Mr. Oakley calls a minimizing Catholicism."

His mind was already made up. So much so that some extremely eloquent and appealing letters written to him by H. P. Liddon, Pusey's closest supporter, had no effect. We learn from one of these letters that Hopkins had put forward what Liddon called "the precarious hypothesis of a personal illumination." But we cannot analyse all the factors which led to this conversion. Though I believe most converts claim to reach supernatural faith by way of reason, Hopkins himself seems to have felt that the gulf between nature and super-nature, between the finite and the infinite, could not be bridged by a process of logic.

The great interests which they shared, Catholicism and poetry, eventually brought Gerard Hopkins and Coventry Patmore into contact, and Patmore paid a tribute to Hopkins at the time of his death which throws a very valuable light on the quality of the faith he held. In a letter to Robert Bridges, Patmore wrote:

"Gerard Hopkins was the only orthodox, and as far as I could see, saintly man in whom religion had absolutely no narrowing effect upon his general opinions and sympathies. A Catholic of the most scrupulous strictness, he could nevertheless see the Holy Spirit in all goodness, truth and beauty; and there was something in all his words and manners which were at once a rebuke and an attraction to all who could only aspire to be like him."

It is important to realise the character of this "freedom in faith" because a consideration of Hopkins's poetry brings us close to a problem which has agitated modern criticism a good deal and which I have already referred to*—I mean the relation of poetry to the poet's beliefs. The problem has been

*See pp. 9-10.

discussed in relation to Dante by Mr. Eliot, and more generally by Mr. Richards in his book on "Practical Criticism." These critics are mainly occupied in discussing whether it is necessary to share a poet's beliefs in order fully to enjoy his poetry. The aspect of the problem that arises in the case of Hopkins is even more vital—the precise effect of a poet's religious beliefs on the nature of his poetry.

II

In Hopkins's poetry, as perhaps in the work of other poets, we can distinguish (1) poetry which is the direct expression of religious beliefs, (2) poetry which has no direct or causal relation to any such beliefs at all, and (3) poetry which is not so much the expression of belief in any strict sense but more precisely of doubt. All Hopkins's poems of any importance can be grouped under these three categories. When this has been done, I think that there would be general agreement that in poetic value the second and third categories are immensely superior to the first. Indeed, so inferior are such strictly religious poems as "Barnfloor and Winepress," "Nondum," "Easter," "Ad Mariam," "Rosa Mystica," and one or two others, that Robert Bridges rightly excluded them from the first edition of the *Poems*. Of the *Poems* published by Dr. Bridges, one or two might conceivably be classified as poems of positive belief, like the exquisite "Heaven-Haven" and "The Habit of

Perfection." "The Wreck of the *Deutschland*," the long poem which Hopkins himself held in such high regard, is a poem of contrition, of fear and submission rather than of the love of God:

> Be adored among men,
>   God, three-numberèd form;
> Wring thy rebel, dogged in den,
>   Man's malice, with wrecking and storm.
> Beyond saying sweet, past telling of tongue,
>   Thou art lightning and love, I found it, a winter and warm;
>   Father and fondler of heart thou hast wrung:
> Hast thy dark descending and most art merciful then.

This is the beauty of terror, the "terrible pathos" of the phrase in which Canon Dixon so perfectly defined Hopkins's quality.

Of the poetry which has no direct or causal relation to beliefs of any kind, poems such as "Penmaen Pool," "The Starlight Night," "Spring," "The Sea and the Skylark," "The Windhover," "Pied Beauty," "Hurrahing in Harvest," "The Caged Skylark," "Inversnaid," "Harry Ploughman," and the two "Echoes," the poetic force comes from a vital awareness of the objective beauty of the world. That awareness—"sensualism," as Dr. Bridges calls it—is best and sufficiently revealed in original metaphors such as "mealed-with-yellow sallows," "piece-bright paling," "daylight's dauphin," "a stallion stalwart, very violet-sweet," and many others of their kind, in which the poet reforges words to match the shape and sharpness of his feelings. Dr. Bridges, in the context I have already quoted from,* speaks of "the naked encounter of sensualism and asceticism which hurts the 'Golden Echo' "—a phrase I cannot in any sense apply to the poem in question; for while I appreciate the magnificent sensualism of this poem, I fail to detect any asceticism in the ordinary secular meaning of the word. But that in general there was a conflict of this sort in Hopkins is revealed, not only by the fact that he destroyed many of his poems which he found inconsistent with his religious discipline, but most clearly in his curious criticism of Keats:

" . . . Since I last wrote, I have re-read Keats a little, and the force of your criticism on him has struck me more than it did. It is impossible not to feel with weariness how his verse is at every turn abandoning itself to an unmanly and enervating luxury. It appears too that he said something like 'O, for a life of impressions instead of thoughts.' It was, I suppose, the life he tried to lead. The impressions are not likely to have been all innocent, and they soon ceased in death. His contemporaries, as Wordsworth, Byron, Shelley, and even Leigh Hunt, right or wrong, still concerned themselves with great causes, as liberty and religion; but he lived in mythology and fairyland, the life of a dreamer: nevertheless, I feel and see in him the beginnings of something opposite to this, of an

*Notes to the *Poems* (Second Edition, Oxford, 1930), pp. 94–99.

interest in higher things, and of powerful and
active thought. . . . His mind had, as it seems to
me, the distinctly masculine powers in abundance,
his character the manly virtues; but, while he gave
himself up to dreaming and self-indulgence, of
course they were in abeyance. Nor do I mean that
he would have turned to a life of virtue—only God
can know that—but that his genius would have
taken to an austerer utterance in art. Reason,
thought, what he did not want to live by, would
have asserted itself presently, and perhaps have
been as much more powerful than that of his
contemporaries as his sensibility or impressionable-
ness, by which he did want to live, was keener and
richer than theirs."

The implication of this criticism is that the poet, by
nature a dreamer and a sensualist, only raises
himself to greatness by concerning himself with
"great causes, as liberty and religion." In what sense
did Hopkins so sublimate his poetic powers? In a
poem like "Pied Beauty" we see the process openly
enacted. After a catalogue of dappled things, things
which owe their beauty to contrast, inconsistency and
change, Hopkins concludes by a neat inversion—an
invocation to God who, fathering forth such things, is
Himself changeless. In "Hurrahing in Harvest"
again we have an extended metaphor: the senses
glean the Saviour in all the beauty of Summer's end.
"The Windhover" is completely objective in its sense-
ful catalogues: but Hopkins gets over his scruples by

dedicating the poem "To Christ our Lord." But this is a patent deception. It does not alter the naked sensualism of the poem; and there is no asceticism in this poem; nor essentially in any of the other poems of this group. They are tributes to God's glory, as all poetry must be; but they are tributes of the senses; and a right conception of God and of religion is not hurt by such tributes.

In the third section, poems expressive not so much of belief as of doubt, I would place those final sonnets, Nos. 40, 41, 44, 45, 46, 47 and 50 in the published *Poems*. These all date from the last years of Hopkins's life—the first six from 1885, the other from 1889, the actual year of his death. But even earlier poems express at least despair: "Spring and Fall"—the blight man was born for; the "Sibyl's Leaves"—the self-wrung rack where thoughts against thoughts grind. But the sonnets themselves are complete in their gloom, awful in their anguish. I need only quote that last terrible sonnet:

Thou art indeed just, Lord, if I contend
With thee; but, sir, so what I plead is just.
Why do sinners' ways prosper? and why must
Disappointment all I endeavour end?

Wert thou my enemy, O thou my friend,
How wouldst thou worse, I wonder, than thou dost
Defeat, thwart me? Oh, the sots and thralls of lust
Do in spare hours more thrive than I that spend,
Sir, life upon thy cause. See, banks and brakes

Now, leavèd how thick! lacèd they are again
With fretty chervil, look, and fresh wind shakes
Them; birds build—but not I build; no, but strain,
Time's eunuch, and not breed one work that wakes.
Mine, O thou lord of life, send my roots rain.

Is there any evidence in the known facts of Hopkins's life which throws light on this state of mind? Father Lahey, in his memoir of Hopkins, speaks of the three sorrows of his last years. The first two were due to external causes and do not concern us here; but Father Lahey then writes:

"Of Hopkins's third sorrow it is more difficult to speak. It sprang from causes which have their origin in true mysticism. Hopkins, smiling and joyful with his friends, was at the same time on the bleak heights of spiritual night with his God. All writers on mysticism—St. Teresa, St. John of the Cross, Poulain, Maumigny, etc.—have told us that this severe trial is the greatest and most cherished *gift* from One Who has accepted literally His servants' oblation. Hopkins was always remembered by all who met him as essentially a priest, a deep and prayerful religious. With the fine uncompromising courage of his initial conversion, he pursued his never-ending quest after spiritual perfection. The celebrated 'terrible' sonnets are only terrible in the same way that the beauty of Jesus Christ is terrible. Only the strong pinions of an eagle can realise the cherished happiness of such suffering. It is a place where Golgotha and Thabor meet. Read in this light his poems cease to be tragic."

The relation of doubt to belief is another and a profounder question than the one which concerns us now. No one who has thought about such matters fails to realise the paradoxical significance of the cry of the dumb child's father: "Lord, I believe; help Thou mine unbelief." As Father Lahey points out, this absence of spiritual complacency is of the very essence of Christian mysticism. An absence of spiritual complacency may also well be of the very nature of poetic sensibility.

Of that psychological aspect of creativity in the poet I have dealt at length in my essay on *Form in Modern Poetry*.* I will only say here, by way of résumé, that we are born with sensibility and come into a world of ready-formulated ideas. As we develop, we may either adapt our sensibility to receive these ideas; or we may painfully create ideas (disciplinary dogmas) which the freely expanding personality can hold in tension. In the latter case the space between self and dogma is *bridged*—there is a bridge, not an abysm of despair—by doubt. My contention is, that a creative gift or poetic sensibility is only consistent with such a state of spiritual tension and acuity. True originality is due to a conflict between sensibility and belief; both exist in the personality, but in counter-action. The evidence is

*Sheed and Ward, London, 1932.

clear to read in all genuine mysticism and poetry; and nowhere more clearly than in the poetry and mysticism of Gerard Hopkins.*

III

The terrible sincerity of the process of Hopkins's thought inevitably led him to an originality of expression which rejected the ready-made counters of contemporary poetics. His originality in this respect is both verbal and metrical, and perhaps the innovations he introduced into metre prevent more than anything else the appreciation of his poetry. Except for a few early poems, which need not be taken into account, practically every poem written by Hopkins presents rhythmical irregularities. The poet himself attempted a theoretical justification of these, and it is an extremely ingenious piece of work. But there can be no possible doubt—and it is important to emphasise this—that the rhythm of Hopkins's poems, considered individually, was intuitive in origin—

> *"Since all the make of man*
> *Is law's indifference."*

The theory was invented later to justify his actual powers. It makes its first appearance in his correspondence in 1877, and in his letters to Bridges and

*Cf. André Gide: "La force poétique aurait-elle décru en moi avec mes sentiments chrétiens. . . . Je ne crois pas; mais plutôt avec ma perplexité. Chacun de mes livres a été, jusqu'à présent, la mise en valeur d'une incertitude." Pages de Journal, p. 665. La Nouvelle Revue Française, May, 1935.

Dixon, Hopkins shows that he understood the technique of English poetry as no poet since Dryden had understood it—Dryden whom he describes so well in one of these letters as "the most masculine of our poets; his style and his rhythms lay the strongest stress of all our literature on the naked thew and sinew of the English language." Such a description looks innocent enough, but it implies the great realisation that poetry must start from the nature of a language—must flow with a language's inflexions and quantities, must, in a word, be *natural*. Such was the secret of Greek poetry, and of Anglo-Saxon poetry; and it is the virtue of most of our poets that they instinctively reject Italianate rhythms, and other foreign impositions, and fall into this natural rhythm, which Hopkins called sprung rhythm. There are many statements and restatements of what he meant by this rhythm in the course of these letters; the best is perhaps that contained in a letter to Canon Dixon (Letter XII).*

"Its principle is that all rhythm and all verse consists of feet and each foot must contain one stress of verse-accent: so far is common to it and Common Rhythm; to this it adds that the stress alone is essential to a foot and that therefore even one stressed syllable may make a foot and consequently two or more stresses may come running, which in

*The Letters of Gerard Manley Hopkins to Robert Bridges. The Correspondence of Gerard Manley Hopkins and Richard Watson Dixon. Edited with notes and an Introduction by Claude Colleer Abbott. (Oxford University Press.) Two volumes, 1935.

common rhythm can, regularly speaking, never happen. But there may and mostly there does belong to a foot an unaccented portion or 'slack': now in common rhythm, in which less is made of stress, in which less stress is laid, the slack must be always one or else two syllables, never less than one and never more than two, and in most measures fixedly one or fixedly two; but in sprung rhythm, the stress being more *of* a stress, being more important, allows of greater variation in the slack and this latter may range from three syllables to none at all—*regularly*, so that paeons (three short syllables and one long or three slacks and one stressy) are regular in sprung rhythm, but in common rhythm occur only by licence; moreover may in the same measure have this range."

The effect of this distinction on the normal conception of poetic measure is revolutionary. Bridges was horrified; Dixon intrigued. "Presumptious jugglery," Bridges called it, misspelling in his indignation. Hopkins replied that he used sprung rhythm "because it is the nearest to the rhythm of prose, that is the native and natural rhythm of speech, the least forced, the most rhetorical and emphatic of all possible rhythms, combining, as it seems to me, opposite and, one would have thought, incompatible excellences, markedness of rhythm— that is rhythm's self—and naturalness of expression." But Bridges was never convinced; I doubt if he ever really saw the point of the discovery—his own later experiments in the measure were feeble; he certainly never realised the importance of it, and the possibility that through Hopkins a renaissance of English poetry would come about would have seemed fantastic to him.

The preface in which he formulates his theories more precisely was written about 1883—in the midst, that is to say, of his main creative period. He begins by saying that his poems are written some in Running Rhythm, by which he means the common rhythm in English use, and some in Sprung Rhythm, and some in a mixture of the two. Common English rhythm, the standard rhythm in use from the sixteenth to the nineteenth centuries, is measured by feet of either two or three syllables and never more or less. Every foot has one principal stress or accent, and for purposes of scanning Hopkins held that it is a great convenience to follow the example of music and take the stress always first, as the accent or chief accent always comes first in a musical bar. If this is done there will be in common English verse only two possible feet—the so-called Trochaic and Dactylic, though these two may sometimes be mixed.

"But because," Hopkins goes on to explain, "verse written strictly in these feet and by these principles will become same and tame, the poets have brought in licences and departures from rule to give variety. . . . These irregularities are chiefly Reversed Feet and Reversed or Counterpoint Rhythm, which two things are two steps or degrees of licence in the same kind."

By a reversed foot, he adds, perhaps unnecessarily, "I mean putting the stress where, to judge from the rest of the measure, the slack should be, and the slack where the stress; and this is done freely at the beginning of the line, and, in the course of a line, after the pause; only scarcely ever in the second foot and never in the last, for these places are characteristic and sensitive and cannot well be touched."

The following two verses from "The Habit of Perfection," one of Hopkins's early poems, show an isolated instance of a reversed foot in the third line; otherwise it is in standard iambic metre:

> *Elected Silence, sing to me*
> *And beat upon my whorlèd ear,*
> *Pipe me to pastures still and be*
> *The music that I care to hear.*
>
> *Shape nothing, lips; be lovely-dumb:*
> *It is the shut, the curfew sent*
> *From there where all surrenders come*
> *Which only makes you eloquent.*

This is, of course, all very simple and unremarkable, and has been the practice of every good poet from Chaucer down: as Hopkins says, it is nothing but the irregularity which all natural growth and motion show.

"If however the reversal is repeated in two feet running, especially so as to include the sensitive second foot, it must be due either to great want of ear or else it is a calculated effect, the super-inducing or *mounting* of a new rhythm upon the old; and since the new or mounted rhythm is actually heard, and at the same time the mind naturally supplies," the standard rhythm which by rights we should be hearing, "two rhythms are in some manner running at once and we have something answerable to counterpoint in music, which is two or more strains of tune going on together, and this is Counterpoint Rhythm. Of this kind of verse Milton is the great master and the choruses of *Samson Agonistes* are written throughout in it."

Let us take a simple example from Hopkins's "God's Grandeur":

The world is charged with the grandeur of God.
It will flame out, like shining from shook foil;
It gathers to a greatness, like the ooze of oil
Crushed. Why do men then now not reck his rod?
Generations have trod, have trod, have trod;
And all is seared with trade; bleared, smeared with toil;
And wears man's smudge and shares man's smell: the soil
Is bare now, nor can foot feel, being shod.

And for all this, nature is never spent;
There lives the dearest freshness deep down things;
And though the last lights off the black West went
Oh, morning, at the brown brink eastward, springs—
Because the Holy Ghost over the bent
World broods with warm breast and with ah! bright
wings.

Here again the underlying measure is standard iambic; but in nearly every line of the sonnet, a foot is reversed and we hear against the running rhythm, this rhythm pointed counter to the proper flow.

If you counterpoint throughout a poem, the original rhythm will be destroyed or lost, and that is actually what happens to the choruses of *Samson Agonistes*. Then the result is what Hopkins calls Sprung Rhythm. It is a rhythm of incomparable freedom: any two stresses may either follow one another running, or may be divided by one, two or three slack syllables. The feet are assumed to be equally long or strong, and their seeming inequality is made up by pause or stressing. Such rhythm cannot be counterpointed. Note also that it is natural for the lines to be *rove over* as Hopkins expressed it, that is, for the scanning of each line immediately to take up that of the one before, so that if the first has one or more syllables at its end, the second must have so many less at its beginning; and in fact the scanning runs on without break from the beginning of a stanza to the end, and all the stanza is one long strain, though written in lines asunder.

Further, Hopkins claims that two licences are natural to Sprung Rhythm. The one is rests, as in music, the other is *hangers* or *outrides*, that is one, two or three slack syllables added to a foot and not counted in the normal scanning. They are so called because they seem to hang below the line or ride forward or backward from it in another dimension

than the line itself. "Felix Randal" is a typical
example of such sprung rhythm:

*Felix Randal the farrier, O he is dead then? my duty all
  ended,*
*Who have watched his mould of man, big-boned and hardy-
  handsome*
Pining, pining, till when reason rambled in it and some
Fatal four disorders, fleshed there, all contended?

*Sickness broke him. Impatient he cursed at first, but
  mended*
*Being anointed and all; though a heavenlier heart began
  some*
Months earlier, since I had our sweet reprieve and ransom
*Tendered to him. Ah well, God rest him all road ever he
  offended!*

This seeing the sick endears them to us, us too it endears,
*My tongue had taught thee comfort, touch had quenched thy
  tears,*
*Thy tears had touched my heart, child, Felix, poor Felix
  Randal;*

*How far from then forethought of, all thy more boisterous
  years,*
*When thou at the random grim forge, powerful amidst
  peers,*
*Didst fettle for the great grey drayhorse his bright and
  battering sandal!*

Hopkins himself, as we have noted, observed that such rhythm is the rhythm of common speech and of written prose, when rhythm is perceived in them; "the least forced, the most rhetorical and emphatic of all possible rhythms, combining, as it seems to me, opposite and, one would have thought, incompatible excellences, markedness of rhythm—that is rhythm's self—and naturalness of expression." It is the rhythm of all but the most monotonously regular music, so that it arises in the words of choruses and refrains and in songs written closely to music. It is found in nursery rhymes, weather saws, and so on; and it arises in common verse when reversed or counterpointed. And I would add, it is the rhythm of all the genuine *vers libre* or free verse which has arisen since Hopkins's time.

This being so, the question arises: how came such a natural and universal rhythm to be neglected in English poetry? Perhaps we should rather ask: how did the standard running rhythm come into existence? and having once come into existence, why did it become such a fixed norm? Not only Greek and Latin lyric verse, which are in sprung rhythm, but the whole tradition of Teutonic and Norse poetry favours the principle of sprung rhythm. So that we may say, that the tradition of sprung rhythm to which Hopkins returned has a tradition within our own linguistic world at least twice as long as the tradition of running rhythm. For running rhythm was only established in England in the sixteenth century, whereas sprung rhythm had existed for at

least eight centuries before that time. Our early
metre is usually known as alliterative, and is entirely
without rhyme. In this metre each line is divided by
a pause, and each half-line contains two or more
stresses, and an irregular number of slacks: the
stresses in each whole line have the same initial
sounds, and on account of this the metre is called
alliterative. The only difference between this metre
and Hopkins's is that Hopkins adds rhyme, and uses
alliteration on no fixed principle. But it will already
have been noticed that he nevertheless makes
considerable use of alliteration. In a few of his
poems the total effect of alliteration is not much less
than in a purely alliterative poem like *Piers Plowman*.
"The Windhover" is a supreme example:

> *I caught this morning morning's minion, king-*
> > *dom of daylight's dauphin, dapple-dawn-drawn Falcon,*
> > > *in his riding*
> > *Of the rolling level underneath him steady air, and*
> > > *striding*
> *High there, how he rung upon the rein of a wimpling wing*
> *In his ecstasy! then off, off forth on swing,*
> > *As a skate's heel sweeps smooth on a bow-bend: the hurl*
> > > *and gliding*
> > *Rebuffed the big wind. My heart in hiding*
> *Stirred for a bird,—the achieve of, the mastery of the thing!*
>
> *Brute beauty and valour and act, oh, air, pride, plume, here*
> > *Buckle! AND the fire that breaks from thee then, a*
> > *billion*

Times told lovelier, more dangerous, O my chevalier!

  No wonder of it: the shéer plód makes plough down
     sillion
Shine, and blue-bleak embers, ah my dear,
  Fall, gall themselves, and gash gold-vermilion.

In short, we might say that Hopkins is eager to use every device the language can hold to increase the force of his rhythm and the richness of his phrasing. Point, counterpoint, rests, running-over rhythms, hangers or outrides, slurs; end-rhymes, internal rhymes, assonance and alliteration—all are used to make the verse sparkle like rich irregular crystals in the gleaming flow of the poet's limpid thought.

The other aspect of his technique is one which, to my way of thinking, is still more central to the poetic reality: I mean his fresh and individual vocabulary. No true poet hesitates to invent words when his sensibility finds no satisfaction in current phrases. Words like "shivelight" and "firedint" are probably such inventions. But most of Hopkins's innovations are in the nature of new combinations of existing words, sometimes contracted similes, or metaphors, and in this respect his vocabulary has a surface similarity to that of James Joyce. Examples of such phrases are to be found in almost every poem: "the beadbonny ash," "fallowbootfellow," "windlaced," "churlsgrace," "footfretted," "clammyish lashtender combs," "wildworth," and so on. Commoner phrases like "beetle-browed," or "star-eyed" are of the same kind, made in the same way, and freely used by him.

Here again an explanation would take us far beyond the immediate subject; for it concerns the original nature of poetry—itself the emotional sound-complex uttered in primitive self-expression. Mr. Williams, whose graceful and appreciative introduction to the second edition of the *Poems* is a fair corrective to the pedantic undertones of Dr. Bridges in the first edition, has an excellent description of the phenomenon as it appeared in the composition of Hopkins's verse.

> "It is as if the imagination, seeking for expression, had found both verb and substantive at one rush, had begun almost to say them at once, and had separated them only because the intellect had reduced the original unity into divided but related sounds."

Poetry can only be renewed by discovering the original sense of word-formation: the words do not come pat in great poetry, but are torn out of the context of experience; they are not in the poet's mind, but in the nature of the things he describes. "You must know," said Hopkins himself, "that words like *charm* and *enchantment* will not do: the thought is of beauty as of something that can be physically kept and lost, and by physical things only, like keys; then the things must come from the *mundus muliebris;* and thirdly they must not be markedly old-fashioned. You will see that this limits the choice of words very much indeed."

Of Hopkins's imagery, there is not much in general to be said, but that "not much" is all. He had that acute and sharp sensuous awareness essential to all great poets. He was physically aware of textures, surfaces, colours, patterns of every kind; aware acutely of earth's diurnal course, or growth and decay, of animality in man and of vitality in all things. Everywhere there is passionate apprehension, passionate expression and equally that passion for form without which these other passions are spend-thrift. But the form is inherent in the passion. "For," as Emerson remarked with his occasional deep insight, "it is not metres, but a metre-making argument, that makes a poem—a thought so passionate and alive, that, like the spirit of a plant or an animal, it has an architecture of its own, and adorns nature with a new thing."

IV*

Hopkins himself was aware of the quality of his genius, and therefore knew what to expect from his contemporaries. Even in his undergraduate days at Oxford, he could write:

"It is a happy thing that there is no royal road to poetry. The world should know by this time that one cannot reach Parnassus except by flying thither. Yet from time to time more men go up and

*In this section I repeat three paragraphs from *Form in Modern Poetry*.

either perish in its gullies fluttering excelsior flags
or else come down again with full folios and blank
countenances. Yet the old fallacy keeps its ground.
Every age has its false alarms."

The most obvious false alarm was Swinburne; but
he was of the number who perish in the gullies of
Parnassus. More false, because more seeming-fair,
are those who come down again with full folios and
blank countenances, and among these can be
numbered some of Hopkins's closest friends. Probably
the only one of his small circle who understood him
fully was his fellow-poet, Richard Watson Dixon.
Canon Dixon, writing to Hopkins to urge him to
write more poems, refers to their quality as "something that I cannot describe, but know to myself by
the inadequate word *terrible pathos*—something of
what you call temper in poetry: a right temper
which goes to the point of the terrible: the terrible
crystal. Milton is the only one else who has anything
like it, and he has it in a totally different way: he has
it through indignation, through injured majesty,
which is an inferior thing . . ." There is a full
understanding which we do not find in the published
letters and writings of others who knew Hopkins—
not in Coventry Patmore, who floundered in deep
astonishment, and not, dare it be said, in his closest
friend and final editor, the late Poet Laureate. To
contend that Dr. Bridges did not understand the
poetry of Hopkins would not be quite fair; he
understood the craftsmanship of it, and was sensible

to the beauty. But there seems to have been an essential lack of sympathy—not of personal sympathy, but of sympathy in poetic ideals. The preface to the notes which Dr. Bridges contributed to the first (1918) edition of the poems, reprinted in the new edition, is marked by a pedantic velleity which would only be excusable on the assumption that we are dealing with a poet of minor interest. That is, indeed, the attitude: please look at this odd fellow whom for friendship's sake I have rescued from oblivion. The emphasis on oddity and obscurity is quite extraordinary, and in the end all we are expected to have is a certain technical interest, leading to tolerance, and the discovery of "rare masterly beauties." Hopkins is convicted of affectation in metaphor, perversion of human feeling, exaggerated Marianism, the "naked encounter of sensualism and asceticism which hurts the 'Golden Echo,' " purely artistic wantonness, definite faults of style, incredible childishness in rhyming—at times disagreeable and vulgar and even comic; and generally of deliberate and unnecessary obscurity. Everything, in such an indictment, must depend on the judge's set of laws, and in criticising Dr. Bridges' treatment of Hopkins, I am wishing to say no more than that the Poet Laureate applied a code which was not that of the indicted. The lack of sympathy is shown precisely in this fact. Hopkins was a revolutionary; that is to say, his values were so fundamentally opposed to current practices, that only by an effort of the imagination could they be comprehended. Once they are comprehended, many apparent faults are justified, and there is no reason to dwell on any of them.

Hopkins was serene and modest in his self-confidence. He could admit the criticism of his friends, and yet quietly persist in his perverseness. To one of them he wrote, in 1879:

"No doubt my poetry errs on the side of oddness. I hope in time to have a more balanced and Miltonic style. But as air, melody is what strikes me most of all in music and design in painting, so design, pattern, or what I call *inscape* is what I, above all, aim at in poetry. Now it is the virtue of design, pattern, or inscape to be distinctive, and it is the vice of distinctiveness to become queer. This vice I cannot have escaped."

And again, a little later:

"Moreover, the oddness may make them repulsive at first sight and yet Lang might have liked them on second reading. Indeed, when, on somebody returning me the *Eurydice*, I opened and read some lines, as one commonly reads whether prose or verse, with the eyes, so to say only, it struck me aghast with a kind of raw nakedness and unmitigated violence I was unprepared for; but take breath and read it with the ears, as I always wish to read, and my verse becomes all right."

In his letters he is revealed as a man of quite exceptional nobility of mind, a man, too, of tender feeling and frank impulsive affection. His real quality was that chastity of mind which he describes in one of his best letters (Letter XCIX to Bridges):

" . . . if a gentleman feels that to be what we call a gentleman is a thing essentially higher than without being a gentleman to be ever so great an artist or thinker or if, to put it another way, an artist or thinker feels that were he to become in those ways ever so great he would still essentially be lower than a gentleman that was no artist and no thinker—and yet to be a gentleman is but on the brim of morals and rather a thing of manners than of morals properly—then how much more must art and philosophy and manners and breeding and everything else in the world be below the least degree of true virtue. This is that chastity of mind which seems to lie at the very heart and be the parent of all other good, the seeing at once what is best, the holding to that, and the not allowing anything else whatever to be even heard pleading to the contrary."

But Hopkins realised that this was "no snatching-matter." "The quality of a gentleman is so very fine a thing that it seems to me one should not be at all hasty in concluding that one possesses it." His own humility was perfect, but he knew that there was an injunction on all poets and artists to let their light shine before men. "I would have you and Canon Dixon and all true poets remember that fame, the being known, though in itself one of the most dangerous things to man, is nevertheless the true and appointed air, element, and setting of genius and its works." For himself it was different; in joining the Society of Jesus he had deliberately renounced fame. In 1881 he told Dixon that he had destroyed all he had written before he entered the Society, and that at first he had meant to write no more. Then his superior suggested that he should write an ode on the wreck of the *Deutschland*, which he did with the results we know. He doubted the wisdom of writing any more poetry unless, so to speak, ordered to do so; but then he came to a compromise: "However I shall, in my present mind, continue to compose, as occasion shall fairly allow, which I am afraid will be seldom and indeed for some years past has been scarcely ever, and let what I produce wait and take its chance; for a very spiritual man once told me that with things like composition the best sacrifice was not to destroy one's work but to leave it entirely to be disposed of by obedience."

It is easy to regret that Hopkins's conscience would not allow him to spend time on poetry, but we must remember that the poet was the man—that his poetic make was complementary to his religious make, and that to ask for a different man is to ask for a different poet. If he had not been a priest, Hopkins would undoubtedly have written more verse— perhaps as much as Bridges or Browning or Swinburne. But he would not necessarily have been a better poet, and as it is, his small harvest is so rich and golden, that we would not exchange it for all the pallid stacks of verse piled up by his contemporaries. Dixon was distressed by the open conflict of religion and poetry, but respected the decision taken by Hopkins. What Bridges thought we do not know, but he had no sympathy for the religious life of his friend, even a definite antipathy. One wonders on what the friendship subsisted, so little were Hopkins's profoundest feelings appreciated by Bridges. But friendship is perhaps never solidly grounded on intellectual interests; Hopkins had known Bridges for ten years before he discovered (and then from a review!) that his friend wrote poetry. We can assume, therefore, that the attraction was instinctive, even physical. How otherwise could Hopkins have tolerated the conceit, the pedantry, the complete lack of perception that were the return for all his frankness, humility and grace? Bridges has cautiously destroyed his side of the correspondence, but that very caution is significant. A man has not such a care for his reputation but from what we call a good conceit of himself, which is a fault even Hopkins found in Bridges.

V

It would be natural to conclude with some estimate of Hopkins's influence on modern poetry. But let us first ask what we should look for under this heading.

The influence of a poet can be either technical, affecting the practice of other poets; or it can be spiritual, affecting the point of view, the philosophy of life, of poets and readers alike. I do not pretend to estimate this second kind of influence in Hopkins's case; and in any event I think it is irrelevant to our strictly poetical enquiry. The acute sensibility of Hopkins has undoubtedly sharpened the perceptive faculties of all who are familiar with his verse; and there may be a few who have felt the profounder truths which he expresses with so much intensity. But such effects would be difficult to estimate. Nor can we come to any very definite conclusion about a technical influence. If by that we mean a mimetic affectation of Hopkins's mannerisms, then the less said about it the better. But the true influence of one poet on another does not show itself so baldly. It may be that in the return to sprung rhythm, in the extended use of alliteration, Hopkins has made a calculable impression on the poets who have been writing during the last ten or fifteen years. But we must remember that although Hopkins's poetry was written fifty years ago, it was not published until 1918. A few of his poems appeared in anthologies a few years earlier, but they were given no prominence, and received no particular attention. The *patent* influence of Hopkins has therefore hardly had time to work itself into the body of English poetry. But the *latent* influence—that is a different question. It is a question of an impregnating breath, breathed into the ear of every poet open to the rhythms of contemporary life,

143

the music of our existence, and the tragedy of our fate. In this sense Hopkins is amongst the most vital poets of our time, and his influence will reach far into the future of English poetry.

OBSCURITY IN POETRY

poetry is a divine instinct and unnatural rage passing the reache of
comen reason.

SPENSER: *Glosse to the Shepheardes Calender.*

ONE of the greatest pleasures of a literary life, to which a reader may be driven by a too close familiarity with the poetry of his own language, and equally by an increasing awareness of the narrow range of creative expression in general, is the exploration of the poetry of another language. This pleasure seems to me to increase with the nearness of a language—its contemporaneity and its consanguinity. I know that the pleasure can be got from a dead language like Latin or Greek; even a schoolboy can be moved by the sonority of Lucretius or by the more liquid sequences of Virgil. The first reading of Dante in the original is a memorable stage in one's poetic education. Racine, in my own experience, is a more uncertain acquisition: I *think* I enjoy the poetic quality of his alexandrines—the grace that rises superior to the monotony—but the apprehension is not so direct and instinctive as I require it to be; as I find it in more recent French poets such as Baudelaire, Laforgue, Rimbaud and most definitely in a poet who has always affected me strangely: Guillaume Apollinaire.

These intimations of poetic essence—for they deserve no stronger name—have never seemed to me to be certain enough to form the basis of a critical opinion, and I think I have always been chary of committing myself when any but the poetry of my native language was concerned. For poetry is such a function of language—almost an impersonal fruit of its slow growth—that it seems contrary to nature that anyone not born to a language should be capable of extracting its essence. I would even go further and suggest that no one whose blood is not coeval and congenital with the language he uses ever attains the last perfection of poetic expression. There is no great *English* poetry written by a Scotsman, a Welshman or an Irishman. Our greatest poets, so far as we know the facts, are singularly pure in their pedigree.

This brings me within distance of racial theories for which I have nothing but contempt. Though I believe that poetic values are the highest values of a culture, I do not connect them with political values; though I would never trust a Scotsman with our poetry, I am quite content to be governed by him; for the life of action and the life of the imagination have nothing in common, to our eternal distress.

It has seemed to me, still speaking from my own experience, that the discovery and appreciation of German poetry is a partial exception to these general observations. I feel sure, at least, that the pleasure I have derived from the gradual discovery of the poetry of a few German poets—Goethe, Hölderlin, George and Rilke—is appreciably different in kind from the sensations accompanying my explorations in other languages. It cannot be altogether due to the fact that my German is self-taught; so, to a large extent (it is also a small extent), are all my languages. And it is useless to suggest that affinity of language can account for the peculiarity of the pleasure: if

the gap between Scots and English cannot be bridged
when the poetic essence is to be reached, how can
we leap from English to German?

In the circumstances I have looked for another
explanation, and think I have found it in the quality
of a particular kind of poetry: for it is only a few
German poets that are concerned, and perhaps in
them I find an enhancement of poetic qualities I
value in English poetry. I cannot find my thrill in
Schiller, nor even in Kleist. Even in Goethe the
pleasure is intermittent; it is only a few of his lyrics
that yield their essence or, to make the metaphor
more exact, that give me the necessary shock. In
these lyrics—and I might equally well for this
purpose take any representative lines from Dante
or Racine or Baudelaire—I experience the poetry
as a direct *impact;* a sensation of sound, and of sound
allied to expressive epithet and metaphor. But in
the case of George and Rilke the sensation is almost
one of sight. Light seems to be involved: a visual
perception. But not a visual perception of the image
alone; rather an intuition of a presence: in Hobbes's
phrase, a sudden glory.

Actually I believe the sensation has to do with the
so-called obscurity of the verse, and is strictly parallel
to the pleasure I derive from obscurity in English
poetry. Rilke in one of his poems cries:

Singe die Gärten, mein Herz, die du nicht kennst;
wie in Glas eingegossene Gärten, klar, unerreichbar.

And that is the perfect analysis of the sensation: the vision of an unknown garden, embedded in glass, clear but unattainable. Vision without meaning, concrete, synthetic, but held in suspense, contemplated without question. But the vision must be won; it is not immediate; it breaks on the concentrated awareness of the reader like a summer dawn. It is the experience which all so-called obscure poetry tries to communicate; but with the rarest success. I am now suggesting that the experience may be obtained from foreign poetry even when that poetry, to a native, may not be particularly obscure. The language acts as an extra veil for the foreigner, and when the veil is penetrated, then he experiences the sudden shock of revelation.

Admittedly, however, this experience is only frequent when the poet in question has a certain tendency towards obscurity even in his own language. Most Germans find Rilke an obscure poet—if only the Rilke of the Duinese Elegies. There is, therefore, a positive value in obscurity which must be affirmed, in opposition to those who expect poetry to be as plain as a pikestaff—or some less obscure object.

Hopkins was fully aware of this quality in poetry, and in one of his letters* describes how it affected him:

"Granted that it [his poem, "The Wreck of the *Deutschland*"] needs study and is obscure, for

Letters of Gerard Manley Hopkins to Robert Bridges (Oxford University Press), 1935. p. 50.

indeed I was not over-desirous that the meaning of all should be quite clear, at least unmistakeable, you might, without the effort that to make it all out would seem to have required, have nevertheless read it so that lines and stanzas should be left in the memory and superficial impressions deepened, and have liked some without exhausting all. I am sure I have read and enjoyed pages of poetry that way. Why, sometimes one enjoys and admires the very lines one cannot understand, as for instance, 'If it were done when 'tis done,' *sqq.*, which is all obscure and disputed, though how fine it is everybody sees and nobody disputes. And so of many more passages in Shakespeare and others."

The empirical argument might be used with good effect—much unquestioned poetry *is* obscure. That Shakespeare is an obscure poet is witnessed, not only by Hopkins, by also the immense libraries of elucidatory criticism which have been devoted to his text. The obscurity is not explained away even by the scholar's usual assumption that anything he cannot understand must be due to a printer's error. The poetry remains in the obscurity—is, in some way, the obscurity itself.* We therefore need some further explanation of the nature of obscurity in poetry.

The germ of a theory of obscurity may be found in the eighteenth-century Italian philosopher, Giam-

*Obscurity should be distinguished from *ambiguity*, which quality has been brilliantly analysed by Mr. Empson in his *Seven Types of Ambiguity* (London, 1930). Ambiguity is essentially *grammatical;* obscurity is *imaginative*. As we shall see, it arises *before* the logical, and therefore grammatical, stage of expression.

battista Vico, and I have already referred to it in my essay on *Form in Modern Poetry*.* Vico's theory, briefly, is that "man, before he has arrived at the stage of forming universals, forms imaginary ideas. Before he reflects with a clear mind, he apprehends with faculties confused and disturbed: before he can articulate, he sings: before speaking in prose, he speaks in verse: before using technical terms, he uses metaphors, and the metaphorical use of words is as natural to him as that which we call natural." The first kind of wisdom in pagan times, Vico says, was *poetic* wisdom—a metaphysic, proceeding not from reasoning or abstraction, as modern philosophy does, but from sensibility and imagination. The metaphysic of such men was poetry, and poetry originated in the necessity of creating a metaphysic —an explanation of the universe. Necessity, we say, is the mother of invention, and invention is another word for imagination. Imagination is a substitute for knowledge—before knowledge was possible, imagination filled the unexplained vacuum created by the questioning existence of man. Naturally such poetry was divine—it invented gods to explain all that was beyond man's power of apprehension, and these gods were clothed in the colours of man's imagination. We may observe the same process in the unfolding minds of children: the poetry of Fairyland. Further, these first men who created gods were called poets, which etymologically means creators. And Vico points out that their creations embodied

*London (Sheed & Ward), p. 37.

the three essentials of great poetry: sublimity, popularity, and the emotional power which renders poetry effective. The very character of poetry, Vico concludes, is precisely this: to render the impossible credible.

From this conception of a poetic *metaphysics*, Vico proceeds to the conception of a poetic *logic*. *Logos* in its original sense meant a fable or an oracle, and poetic logic is the elaboration of a myth. Out of this poetic logic, as a necessary result, came the metaphor, to this day the most common of all poetic tropes. It originated in mythology, which endowed inanimate things with human sentiments and passions. A metaphor is a shorthand fable. It is a fable summarised in a phrase, and it still retains all the irrationality of its origins. The simplest metaphors relate inanimate things to the human body, or to human actions: *mouth* for any opening, the *teeth* of a saw or a comb, a *tongue* of land, the *gorge* of a mountain, a *handful* for a small number, *heart* for the middle of anything, the *flesh* of a fruit; the wind *whistles*, and so on. Many other "figures of speech" have a similar pre-logical origin, but so much is obvious. All I want to emphasise is the fact that Vico establishes the priority of poetic logic, or the logic of the imagination, and differentiates it in kind from the logic of prose, which is the logic of reasoning.

Vico's theory was first published in 1725 and though it is not often acknowledged, I fancy a consciousness of it was gradually diffused among critics during the eighteenth century and was the beginning of that movement in criticism sometimes associated with romanticism, but which it is preferable to call empirical criticism in opposition to that *a priori* criticism based on the pedantic tradition of classicism. We find a consciousness of it, I think, in Thomas Warton's commentary on Milton's shorter poems, first published in 1785, a landmark in the history of English criticism. Warton, for example, commenting incidentally upon the image of Satan in *Paradise Lost*, Book IV:

> *His stature reached the sky, and on his crest*
> *Sate HORROR plum'd.—*

criticises his pedantic predecessor, Dr. Newton, for regarding the passage as an extravagant metaphor in which "Horror is personified and made the plume of his helmet." "Other and better explanations might be offered," suggests Warton. "But, I believe, we have no precise or determinate conception of what Milton means. And we detract from the sublimity of the passage in endeavouring to explain it, and to give a distinct signification. Here is a nameless terrible grace, resulting from a mixture of ideas, and a confusion of imagery."*

That Coleridge was conscious of Vico's theories, or arrived unconsciously at similar ideas, as he seems to have had a habit of doing, might be easily demonstrated. But it would serve me better to quote Coleridge as a poet rather than as a critic. A poem

*Poems, etc., ed. T. Warton. 2nd ed., 1791, p. 505.

154

like "The Ancient Mariner" is full of obscurities. Indeed, we might say of Coleridge's poetry in general, that its poetic worth is in inverse ratio to its logical sense, reaching its greatest intensity in the incoherent imagery of "Kubla Khan."

Henri Bergson, who may perhaps be regarded as the culmination of the anti-Cartesian movement of thought initiated by Vico, gives a convincing description of the poetic activity in his last book.* He is investigating the nature of mysticism, and turns first to the musician for an analogy. What, he asks, could be more constructive, more scientific than a symphony of Beethoven's? But in addition to his work of arrangement and rearrangement, his selection, which is carried out on the intellectual plane, the composer projects himself to a point beyond this scheme and there he seeks the final direction or inspiration: and this point is an emotional complex which the intelligence can help to resolve into musical terms, but which in itself is more than music and more than intelligence. And so with the inspired writer, be he poet or mystic. He projects himself beyond the region of the concepts and words in which the normal thought processes are expressed. He reaches beyond this plane to a point where the mind feels a pressing need for creation. The existence of this need has only to be plainly felt once in a lifetime, but it will always be there, a unique emotion, an impulse or urge received from the very base of things. To obey it incontinently, it is necessary to forge words, to

*Les deux sources de la morale et de la religion (Paris, 1932), pp. 270 ff.

155

create ideas, but this means to abandon communication, and therefore writing. But the poet attempts to achieve the impossible. He will seek the essential emotion, the form which wants to create its matter, and with this he will confront the ready-made ideas, already existing words, stereotyped notions of reality. In the process he will feel the form becoming explicit in symbols of its own creation, fragments of its own materialisation. But how can these elements, each unique of its kind, be made to square with words already expressive of things? It becomes necessary to violate words, to do violence to such elements. Still success will never be assured: the poet is continually asking himself whether he is justified in going to extremes; every partial success depends on chance. But if he succeeds, he achieves a thought capable of taking on a new aspect for every new generation— he enriches humanity with a capital sum which is not spent at once, but goes on earning interest indefinitely.

To the evidence of the philosopher we may add that of a philosophical poet, Paul Valéry. A disciple of Mallarmé, a metaphysician and a scientist, he has given us the most penetrating criticism of the art of poetry that has been written in our time. I choose as a recent statement of his views an article he contributed to the *Nouvelle Revue Française* in May, 1932. It is most apt for my purpose. It is an article devoted to Mallarmé and even to this very question of obscurity which is raised so acutely by Mallarmé's poetry. Valéry begins by deploring the facility demanded by the reading public; for his part, he requires a power of resistance in a book, and a capacity in the reader to match the care and zeal of the writer with corresponding virtues of patience, leisure, and distinct and deliberate attention. He refutes the notion that complexity or obscurity is to be dismissed as romanticism. Romanticism is afraid of ideas, of the process of thought involved in this mode of creation, and relies for its effect on descriptive epithets, contrasts of detail, "jewelled" words. But Mallarmé advances far beyond such a method; we feel in his verse the presence and the firm design of abstract thought.

But I must not follow Valéry in his particular views on Mallarmé's poetry; I am concerned with certain general ideas which he enunciates. He describes how this least primitive of poets nevertheless acquires the most powerful quality of primitive poetry: its magical formula, its quality of incantation, and he has a finely emotive paragraph claiming that the very efficacy of such poetry depends on the obscurity of the words used:

"What is sung or articulated in the most solemn and the most critical moments of life; what we hear in a Liturgy; what is murmured or groaned in the extremity of passion; what calms a child or the afflicted; what attests the truth of an oath—these are words of a particular tone and expression which cannot be resolved into clear ideas, nor separated out, without making them absurd or silly. In all these cases, the accent and inflexion of the voice outweigh anything intelligible conveyed to us: it is our life rather than our mind which is addressed.— I would say that such words incite us to *become*, rather than excite us to *understand*."

This, of course, is to resort to the magical apology for poetry, deplored by scientific critics like Mr. Empson. But M. Valéry does not stay there. He proceeds, in fact, to adopt Vico's theory, without any acknowledgment, and perhaps unconsciously. Poetry, he says, goes back to some stage of human development anterior to writing and criticism. "I find," he adds, "a very ancient man in every true poet; he still drinks at the source of language; he invents 'verses'—just as the most gifted primitive man had to invent 'words,' or the ancestors of words." Most people are deaf to the words they use: their words are expedients necessary for expression, and they use them in a purely practical spirit. "But poetry remains pagan: for every soul it requires a body—there is no meaning, no idea which is not an issue of some remarkable figure of speech, made up of tones, intervals, and intensities. . . .

". . . the *given* language acquired in childhood, being of a statistical and communal origin, is generally not well fitted to express shades of thought far from practical: such a language scarcely lends itself to ends more profound or more precise than those which determine the actions of everyday life. Therefore technical languages come into being—and among the literary language. In all languages sooner or later a *mandarin's language* appears, sometimes far removed from the customary language; but generally this literary language is derived from the other, from which it draws words, figures of speech, and phrases best fitted to express the effects which the literary artist aims at. Thus it happens that some writers make up a language of their own. . . . Mallarmé created a language almost entirely his own by a refined choice of words and by using exceptional turns of speech which he invented or adapted, always refusing the immediate solution suggested to him on every side. And this is no more than defending himself, precisely in the details and elementary functioning of mental life, *against automatism*."

We see therefore, essentially that obscurity lies not in the poet, but in ourselves. We are clear and logical at the cost of being superficial or inexact. The poet, more exactingly, seeks absolute precision of language and thought, and the exigences of this precision demand that he should exceed the limits of customary expression, and therefore *invent*—invent sometimes words, more frequently new uses of words, most frequently phrases and figures of speech which re-animate words, and among these, above all, *metaphor*. Metaphor, in fact, for such a poet becomes the normal mode of expression, and I think we should always be prepared to judge a poet, to the exclusion of all other qualities, by the force and originality of his metaphors.

I must be quite clear what I mean by metaphor. Originally, no doubt, as Vico suggests, the metaphor arose from the habit of ascribing the attributes of the human organism to inanimate objects. The name implies a transference of attributes, and the ordinary dictionary definition of a metaphor is "the application of a name or descriptive term to an object to which it is not literally applicable (e.g. *a glaring error*)." Such a conception is very inadequate for the uses of poetry. We might define metaphor summarily as the discovery of an illuminating correspondence between two objects, but that too is inadequate for the subtleties of the process. In fact, the modern poet has passed beyond the metaphor to a new figure of speech. This has been called the *image*—"The image," writes a modern French poet, Paul Reverdy, "is a pure creation of the mind. It cannot emerge from a comparison but only from the bringing together of two more or less distant realities. . . . An image is not striking because it is brutal or fantastic—but because the association of ideas is remote and exact. . . . No image is produced by comparing (always inadequately) two disproportionate realities. A striking image, on the contrary, one new to the mind, is produced by bringing into relation without comparison two distant realities whose relations *the mind alone* has seized."

Jacques Maritain, with particular reference to Reverdy's definition,* notes that the image thus conceived is the opposite of *metaphor*, which compares one known thing with another known thing the better to express the former by covering it with the

Art and Scholasticism (London, 1930), p. 192.

latter. The image *discovers* one thing with the help of another, and by their resemblance makes the unknown known. But it is not a logical resemblance. As a modern philologist, Karl Vossler, says in another connection* (he is dissecting the image of the "shining moon"—in Latin there was a connection between the two words *luceo* and *luna*, but no one knows whether a "shining moon" or a "moon-like shine" came first, whether the moon entered into the shining or the shining into the moon), "linguistic comparisons of this kind are not logical acts of thought at all. They are the dream of a poet, in which things come together, not because they are being differentiated or because they are being identified, but because they are thought and felt together in an emotional unity."

I halt on the threshold of philology, for finally it is to the philosophy of language that this enquiry leads us, to the most interesting and fundamental of all sciences. An affirmation of obscurity in poetry must force on us a reconsideration of the function of language. Obscurity in poetry cannot be regarded as merely a negative quality, a failure to attain a state of perfect clarity. It is a positive value, but more, it is a whole series of such values. Apart from the pure and unmeaning sound-value of words, and apart from their irrational magic, their power of incantation—aspects of the question I have not thought worth more than a mention—there is a fundamental obscurity in the actual thought process

The Spirit of Language in Civilisation (London, 1933).

involved—an obscurity due to the honesty and objectivity of the poet. He works outwards from an emotional unity. This unity may be clothed in what Vossler calls "an inner language form"; but between this inner language form and the outer language form in which our everyday rational thoughts are expressed, there is no necessary correspondence. In order to remain faithful to the inner language form, the poet must invent words and create images, he must mishandle and stretch the meaning of words. The emotional unity of the poem is given; the correspondence in words must be created; and that is why the poet is called a creator.

It is a mistake, therefore, to ask a poet to explain his poems. That is to make the wrong approach to poetry, to knock at the wrong door. This emotional unity which is the *raison d'être* of every poem cannot be measured by the instruments of reason. Otherwise it would be simpler to express it in prose. The poem must be received directly, without questioning, and loved or hated. It has a necessary and eternal existence; it is impervious to reason, and if it has no discoverable meaning, it has immeasurable power. The poet has created in words an objective equivalence of his emotional experience: the words may not make sense, but they make the emotion— follow the contour of the thought—and reproduce, as nearly as possible, "the mind's internal echo of the imperfect sound." It was Rilke who said that "the poet is farther away from men than from things." That is perhaps why he seems so strange to us. But the things he approaches are eternal things, and because they endure in his words, his words grow familiar to men, until they are accepted without questioning, but always with fresh recognition.

TWO NOTES ON SWIFT*

*To be considered as addenda to my essay on Swift in *The Sense of Glory* (Cambridge University Press, 1929).

I.—SWIFT'S POETRY.

ON this subject everyone knows Dryden's famous remark, repeated by Johnson: "Cousin Swift, you will never be a poet." This was justly inspired by a certain Pindaric Ode written to the "Athenian Society," which begins in this strain:

> *As when the deluge first began to fall,*
> *That mighty ebb never to flow again,*
> *When this huge body's moisture was so great,*
> *It quite o'ercame the vital heat;*
> *That mountain which was highest, first of all*
> *Appear'd above the universal main,*
> *To bless the primitive sailor's weary sight;*
> *And 'twas perhaps Parnassus, if in height*
> *It be as great as 'tis in fame,*
> *And nigh to Heaven as is its name;*
> *So, after the inundation of a war,*
> *When Learning's little household did embark,*
> *With her world's fruitful system, in her sacred ark,*
> *At the first ebb of noise and fears,*
> *Philosophy's exalted head appears. . . .*

There is no sensible quickening of this pedestrian pace anywhere else in the Ode, which is long and desperately wearisome; there is not a single line with which a partisan of Swift could challenge Dryden's judgment. But the Ode was written by a young man of twenty-four; the Pindaric style was imposed upon him by the fashion of the time; and had he never written in another style, he would never have out-lived Dryden's damnation.

But we cannot be sure that this side of Swift's genius is properly appreciated even now, with the whole bulk of his verse before us. That bulk is considerable (more than 750 pages of Bohn's Standard Library), and there is no doubt that Swift was a poet in his own estimation. In the estimation of others he has not fared so well. Goldsmith was willing to place him for poetic genius in the same rank as Milton, Dryden and Pope; but the more representative estimate for the eighteenth century is that of Johnson:

> "In the Poetical Works of Dr. Swift there is not much upon which the critick can exercise his powers. They are often humorous, almost always light, and have the qualities which recommend such compositions, easiness and gaiety. They are, for the most part, what their author intended. The diction is correct, the numbers are smooth, and the rhymes exact. There seldom occurs a hard-laboured expression, or a redundant epithet; all his verses exemplify his own definition of a good style, they consist of *proper words in proper places*."

The only critic who has since dared to qualify this Johnsonian estimate is Taine, whose nationality perhaps secured for him the necessary detachment.

Taine, it is true, is still impeded by a certain pre-
supposition about the nature of poetry; but who,
among the critics of a romantic age, is free? "Ce qui
manque le plus à ses vers c'est la poésie. L'esprit
positif ne peut ni l'aimer ni l'entendre; il n'y voit
qu'une machine ou une mode, et ne l'emploie que
par vanité ou convention. . . . Je ne me rappelle
pas une seule ligne de lui qui indique un sentiment
vrai de la nature; il n'apercevait dans les forêts que
des bûches et dans les champs que des sacs de grain."
But if he could fall into this error (which we shall
comment on presently) Taine could in return appreciate those aspects of genius which transcend
academic distinctions, and cry out his admiration in
these magnificent terms:

"Mais, dans les sujets prosaïques, quelle vérité et
quelle force! Comme cette mâle nudité rabaisse
l'élégance cherchée et la poésie artificielle d'Addi-
son et de Pope! Jamais d'épithètes; il laisse sa
pensée telle qu'elle est, l'estimant pour elle-même
et pour elle seule, n'ayant besoin ni d'ornements,
ni de préparations, ni d'allongements, élevé au-
dessus des procédés de métier, des conventions
d'école, de la vanité de rimailleur, des difficultés
de l'art, maître de son sujet et de lui-même. Cette
simplicité et ce naturel étonnent en des vers. Ici,
comme ailleurs, son originalité est entière et son
génie créateur; il dépasse son siècle classique et
timide; il s'asservit la forme, il la brise, il y ose
tout dire, il ne lui épargne aucune crudité. Recon-

naissez la grandeur dans cette invention et dans
cette audace; celui-là seul est un homme supérieur
qui trouve tout et ne copie rien."

Magnificent!   But not altogether true.   For this
picture of a giant breaking through all bonds, scorn-
ing all obstructions, master of his subject and of
himself, is a romantic half-truth.   In reality, before
he can be master of himself and of his subject this
giant must forge new chains.   He cannot break an
old form without finding himself under the necessity
of creating a new one; and the grandeur and audacity
of the poet Swift lie not in his lack of all convention,
but in his discovery of a new one.   He found the
Pindaric style uncongenial to the substance of his
inspiration; for him it had no meaning and no sympathetic appeal.   If he had meekly accepted Dryden's
reproof he would never have written another verse.
But he realised that although he might not be a poet
in Dryden's sense, the poetry within him was too
real to be refused expression.

Dryden died when Swift was only thirty-three.   It
is just possible that he may have seen "Mrs. Frances
Harris's Petition," which is one of the first of Swift's
poems in an original manner.   If so, it is difficult to
believe that in his wise tolerance he would not have
recognised its kinship with Chaucer, whom he
praised so greatly.   Mrs. Harris is as vivid as the
Wife of Bath, and the verses in which she lives are
a miracle of humorous invention.   It must be admitted
that we never find in Swift that "rude sweetness of

a Scotch tune" which Dryden rather grudgingly allowed to Chaucer, but in the poems which we would make the basis of an apology for him, the very accents of human speech are imposed upon the rhythm, giving it an actuality in which mere sweetness is transcended. It is doubtful whether Dryden would have admitted this quality into his poetic code, for with all his tolerance he reverted always to certain abstract categories against which he judged present performances. Of his English predecessors he was always ready to insist "the times were ignorant in which they lived." Of much of Shakespeare that we habitually admire, he would remark: "What a pudder is here kept in raising the expression of trifling thoughts."

Dryden's is the finest expression in English criticism of what we may term a traditional classicism. But there is another type of classicism, not necessarily an alternative type, which must be briefly delineated before we can justify Swift's right to the name of poet. We would call it a natural classicism, and it arises precisely from that effort to find new forms to match new substances for which Swift is notable. Dryden's abstract categories of verse were based on the best classical models; the problem was, how to mould our rough island speech into these golden numbers. But it is possible to conceive another kind of abstraction which is based on the inherent qualities of the poetic substance: the form is inherent in the substance, and the problem is one of elucidation.

There is no evidence that Swift ever posed the

problem in this categorical manner, but the moral of "The Battle of the Books," if it has one, tends in this direction. Ancient and Modern are terms conveying no necessary virtue; all alike must be submitted to a clear judgment, and the same judgment prevails in the act of composition. It is the presence of judgment, with the purpose of fitting form to substance, that determines the classical quality of the poet's work. The first instructions which Swift gives to "a young beginner" in that ironic masterpiece, "On Poetry—a Rhapsody," are meant seriously enough:

> Consult yourself; and if you find
> A powerful impulse urge your mind,
> Impartial judge within your breast
> What subject you can manage best;
> Whether your genius most inclines
> To satire, praise, or humorous lines,
> To elegies in mournful tone,
> Or prologue sent from hand unknown.
> Then, rising with Aurora's light,
> The Muse invoked, sit down to write;
> Blot out, correct, insert, refine,
> Enlarge, diminish, interline;
> Be mindful, when invention fails,
> To scratch your head, and bite your nails.

There can be no doubt that Swift found in himself a powerful impulse to write verse, and though at first, as we have seen, he attempted a form not suited to his genius, he soon abandoned these artificial exercises. The forms that he then adopted he made essentially his own. In his introduction to the essay which he devoted to Swift's verse* the late Dr. Elrington Ball remarked that "no exact prototype is to be found for Swift's style of versification. It has been described as Hudibrastic, but the influence of Samuel Butler was only partial. In its construction Swift laid under contribution all classes of metrical composition from the Elizabethan age to his own, ephemeral songs and ballads no less than the standard writings of poets and dramatists." We have already quoted Johnson's testimony to the technical perfection of Swift's verse, and indeed that has never been in question. It is the substance which we are called upon to justify.

Goldsmith said that Swift was the first poet who dared to describe nature as it is with all its deformities, and to give exact expression to a turn of thought alike dry, sarcastic and severe. It was for this courage that he placed him in the same rank as Milton, Dryden and Pope. This shows that the poet of "The Deserted Village" had none of the prejudices about the nature of poetry which have distinguished many other poets and critics in the presence of Swift's verse. The assumption of such people is that poetry connotes but one half of life—things of beauty, sentiments of pleasure, innocence of experience. This is the attitude represented by *The Golden Treasury*, a justly famous anthology which has nevertheless done

*Swift's Verse. An Essay, by F. Elrington Ball, Litt.D. (London: Murray, 1929.)

more to prevent a catholic appreciation of English poetry than any other single book or influence. Its sub-title "Of the best Songs and Lyrical Poems" is always ignored; "Lyrical" is silently equated with "poetical." There is an ironic justice in the fact that the only poem in the volume which reflects in any realistic manner the darker aspects of life should contain the lines—

> *Make no deep scrutiny*
> *Into her mutiny.*

But that is just what Swift was bent on doing. His whole life was one long mutiny—mutiny against the darkness of fate, the injustice of men, the baseness of our natural instincts, the indignity of our bodily functions—and his work is one long scrutiny into these dark depths. It is possible to say that Swift's reaction to life was morbid. Mr. Ellis Roberts recently expressed this point of view in an interesting essay which he published with a selection of Swift's poems.* He says:

"In this matter Swift exhibits all the signs of an enormous neurasthenia. To the neurasthenic anything which comes regularly and in routine is liable to become intolerable. Not all of life, fortunately, will so change its character, Different sufferers will become victims of different fears. . . . With Swift it was, at last, always this one thing.

Miscellaneous Poems, by Jonathan Swift, D.D. Edited by R. Ellis Roberts; decorated with Engravings on Wood, by Robert Gibbings. (The Golden Cockerel Press, 1928.)

The boudoir, the closet, the double bed. . . his fancy only has to stray to one of them—and it strayed far too often—and he writhes helpless, indignant, outraged, in pangs which make him for ever of the company of those artists who pace, like the damned souls whom Vathek saw on the fiery and reverberating pavements of hell, each with his hand over his heart, and each with a heart of burning flame."

Mr. Roberts in another place in his essay says of Swift that "he does not delight in filth, as Rabelais; nor has he the curiosity, intellectual, sombre, enragedly humorous, into sexual life which marks Mr. James Joyce's work; Swift's attitude is one of plain, simple, immediate reaction."   Both these statements are true in intention, and so far illuminating; their fault is that they conjure up, in a slight degree, the romantic giant of Taine's invention. They do not, that is to say, sufficiently convey the cool deliberateness of Swift's pen. The man who wrote "A Beautiful Young Nymph Going to Bed," "The Progress of Marriage," "The Lady's Dressing Room," "Strephon and Chloe," and other such grim pieces was certainly indignant, but he was not helpless.   He was always, in Taine's words, "maître de son sujet et de lui-même." If he had a tendency to be neurasthenic (and what man of sensibility is free from it?), then it is more than likely that in his poetry he purged himself of this anguish. But is it possible, the reader of *The Golden Treasury* may ask, to dignify

175

with the name of poetry such dross of a diseased sensibility?

To this question we must answer, that the relations of art to life are so intricate that they do not permit of a neat separation into categories. It is impossible to define art by its substance; it is impossible to define it by its form. All we can say is that substance determines form, and that if from the substance we can proceed to the form, then the work of art is in being. The power needed to pass from substance to form, from matter to essence, is the specific creative impulse, an intense awareness of sensibility in the individual. The direction of this power is arbitrary; that is to say, it depends on the particular environment or constitution of the individual, and one might as well complain of the varieties of colour given by the light of the sun, as of the varieties of art reflected by the mind of man.

II.—THE TREASON OF A CLERK.

There is a general difficulty in any critical approach to Swift's work which this note is only intended to raise, not to solve: the temerity of any purely literary judgment. If we make a distinction between contingent literature and absolute literature—between authors who only write when there is a public and external stimulus and authors whose stimulus is subjective, who write because they enjoy writing as a free and creative activity—then we shall see that the whole of Swift's work is contingent. He is, on a grand scale, an occasional writer; even *Gulliver's Travels*, the most absolute of his works, is determined by his political experience; it is a final judgment on humanity, but not on the abstract humanity of history and philosophy, but on the mass of human beings contemporary with the author. All that Swift wrote is empirical, experiential, *actuel*. It is impossible to detach it from circumstances; we must consider each book or pamphlet in relation to its political intention. It is true that the world has refused to do this in the case of *Gulliver*, but the world's appreciation of *Gulliver* is not critical, not exact. We cut the slings and blunt the arrows of that angry onslaught; we dull the deadly mirror with the moist breath of our complacency.

Nevertheless, though none of Swift's works can be separated from its historical occasion, historical considerations cannot usurp æsthetic judgment. Nor are we at liberty to assume that Swift himself would have resented the application of a purely literary standard to his writings. In a "Letter to a Young Gentleman lately enter'd into Holy Orders," Swift laid the greatest emphasis on literary accomplishment. In that pamphlet occurs his famous "true definition of style"—"proper Words in proper Places"; and there he urges the study of the *English* language—"the neglect whereof is one of the most general Defects among the Scholars of this Kingdom." After warning the novice against pedantry and vulgarity, he selects two especial defects for mention:

177

"the first is the Frequency of flat unnecessary Epithets, and the other is the Folly of using old thread-
bare Phrases, which will often make you go out of
your Way to find and apply them, are nauseous to
rational Hearers, and will seldom express your
Meaning as well as your own natural Words. . . .
When a Man's Thoughts are clear, the properest
Words will generally offer themselves first, and his
own Judgment will direct him in what Order to
place them, so they may best be understood. . . .
In short, that Simplicity without which no human
Performance can arrive to any great Perfection, is
nowhere more eminently useful than in this."

All this shows a high literary conscience; and the
same quality is betrayed in the very interesting
references to the composition of *Gulliver's Travels*
which occur in his letters to Ford.* On January 19,
1723-4, he writes: "My greatest want here is of somebody qualified to censure and correct what I write,
I know not above two or three whose Judgment I
would value, and they are lazy, negligent, and without any Opinion of my Abilityes." Then in a letter
of November 20, 1733, referring to Motte's edition,
he writes: "Had there been onely omissions, I should
not care one farthing; but change of Style, new things
foysted in, that are false facts, and I know not what,
is very provoking. . . . Besides, the whole Sting is
taken out in severall passages, in order to soften them.

The Letters of Jonathan Swift to Charles Ford. Edited by David
Nichol Smith. (Oxford: Clarendon Press. London: Milford, 1935.)

Thus the Style is debased, the humor quite lost, and the matter insipid." Other references to the composition of *Gulliver* show that it was first written in rough draft, then amended, and finally completely transcribed by the author.

Swift's literary conscience thus established, we might next inquire whether he considered himself as primarily a writer, as an author rather than a clergyman or a politician; whether he considered himself as of the same "trade" as his cousin Dryden or his friends Pope and Gay. Such an inquiry touches on one of the mysteries of Swift's life—his attitude towards religion in general and his holy orders in particular. That difficult problem must for the present be evaded, though incidentally a sentence in a letter to Ford of June 22, 1736, should be noted: "I have long given up all hopes of Church or Christianity." The problem can be evaded because a career as author is not inconsistent with a career in the Church—both ends can be pursued concurrently, as many careers testify (Newman's, for example). If we are charitable, and assume that Swift took orders for more than worldly motives; if we make the still more generous assumption that his political activities were based on a disinterested idealism; even then we can still ask: Did Swift consider himself as first and foremost an author? Was his highest ambition literary—was he, not merely a clergyman, but also, in the medieval sense of the word and in Julien Benda's modern sense, a clerk?

It is at any rate illuminating to reconstruct Swift's

life from this point of view—to regard him as essentially what we should call an "intellectual," and to see in his various strivings nothing but the desire of an intellectual to secure himself an economic competency and an assured position on which he could base a life of disinterested intellectual activity—a life of scholarship, as he would probably have called it. It will be remembered how much he hankered after the post of Historiographer Royal, and how scornful he was when it went to an obscure (though competent) archæologist. In a letter to Lord Peterborough, written in 1711 when his political career was yet full of promise, Swift said: "My ambition is to live in England, and with a competency to support me with honour," and there is no reason to doubt the sincerity of that modest ambition. But some of his letters to Ford, written with more obvious sincerity, are still more revealing. Later in this same year 1711 he wrote:

"Now to your former Letter, where you say the Publick requires my Leisure. The Publick is a very civil Person, and I am it's humble Servant, but I shall be glad to shake hands with it as soon as I can. . . . You are in the right as to my Indifference about Irish affairs, which is not occasioned by my Absence, but contempt of them; and when I return my Indifference will be full as much. I had as live be a Beau in Dublin as a Politician, nay, I had as lieve be an Author there; and if ever I have any thoughts of making a Figure in that Kingdom, it shall be at Laracor. I will talk Politicks to the Farmers, and publish my Works at Trim."

Later, in 1719, when his high ambitions for place and power had been disappointed, when he was irrevocably condemned to a deanery in Dublin, he wrote to his friend a little more ruefully, but still in the same strain:

"You know I chuse all the sillyest Things in the World to amuse my self, in an evil age, and a late time of life, ad fallendam canitiem quae indies obrepit. Little trifling Businesses take up so much of my time, that I have little left for speculation, in which I could gladly employ my self, for my Eyes begin to grudge (that I may speak in Royall Style) me reading, and the Pen is not half so troublesom. But instead of that, I do everything to make me forget my self and the World as much as I can."

About a month later he confesses to Ford that "it would be an admirable Scituation to be neither Whig nor Tory. For a Man without Passions might find very strong Amusements." A Man without Passions —party passions, national passions, religious passions —that is the definition of the true clerk, the intellectual, the scholar. One can admire Swift only this side idolatry and still regret that this "indifference," this sublime rational sentiment, had been his earlier in life. For he found that "the turn of Blood at 50" disposed him strongly to fears; he had lost his equanimity, as Wood's halfpence were soon to prove. But in the midst of his fears he was struggling for serenity, and through the course of *Gulliver's Travels* we see him gradually achieving it. They were finished, revised and transcribed in his country cabin at Quilca, among the bogs and rocks. His last Voyage was to a race "whose grand Maxim is, to cultivate *Reason*, and to be wholly governed by it." "Neither is *Reason* among them a Point problematical as with us, where Men can argue with Plausibility on both sides of a Question; but strikes you with immediate Conviction; as it needs must do where it is not mingled, obscured, or discoloured by Passion and Interest." But it was a man already broken in health, weary of nerve and empty of love, who made this discovery; leaving us to wonder that in such extremity such a masterpiece could be written.

DIDEROT'S LOVE LETTERS

DIDEROT'S LOVE LETTERS.

DIDEROT's letters to Sophie Volland have been called the greatest love letters in the world; and though this description is vague enough to mean nothing in particular, yet it is difficult to think of any other correspondence of this nature so sustained in duration and intensity. The three volumes which M. Babelon recently edited for the first time after the original manuscripts* run to nearly a thousand pages; and yet they represent only a third of the original correspondence. The letters were numbered consecutively by each writer, as a check against the uncertainties of the post; the last letter of Diderot's which has survived, written from The Hague in September, 1774, is No. 553. Not a single letter of Sophie Volland's survives; of Diderot's M. Babelon has been able to assemble 187, and there are in addition thirty pages of fragments, selected by Diderot's friend, Jacques André Naigeon, who published a complete edition of the Encyclopædist's works in 1798.

If we were concerned with ordinary love letters we might cry: Enough! The pretty nonsense which most lovers indulge in when they write to one another

*Denis Diderot: *Lettres à Sophie Volland.* Edited by André Babelon. Three Volumes. (Paris: Librairie Gallimard, 1930.)
Denis Diderot: *Correspondance Inédite.* Edited by André Babelon. Two Volumes. (Paris: Librairie Gallimard, 1931.)

is consecrated by the passion which occasions it; to the outsider, unless he can bring to it the vicarious warmth of his own consenting feelings, it is apt to seem like ashes that have lost their glow. Lovers absorbed in themselves and in each other forget the world; they narrow their interests to a point, and even if they are in themselves interesting personalities, as we may grant Elizabeth Barrett and Robert Browning to have been, the interest of their correspondence expires in the heat of its own concentrated focus. The interest, the vivacity and the charm of Diderot's letters to Sophie Volland are due to the very opposite quality, to the fact that he offers to Sophie, not merely the reflection of his passion, but the sum of all his interests, the whole man. And in Diderot's case the man was the age. Perhaps only Voltaire can be suggested as a more representative figure: his range was greater, but it may be doubted whether he shared the life of the period so intimately. An ironic spirit always stands apart; Diderot loved his fellow-men even to the degree of sentimentality.

Louise Henriette Volland, known to her friends as Sophie, exists only in the correspondence of Diderot. She played no part, as was otherwise the fashion with the *femme philosophe* of the time, in the social life which Diderot himself lived so fully. The official archives record her birth (on November 27, 1716) and her death (on February 22, 1784), but every other detail about her we must reconstruct as best we can from Diderot's letters. We learn that she was delicate, which may well have been the reason why she never left her own family circle, that she wore spectacles, and that she had a passion for ices. Of scarcely a single other trait have we definite information, and the two portraits which Diderot mentions from time to time have disappeared. One of them, characteristically enough, was painted on the flyleaf of his Horace, and perished with his library in Russia. But one cannot read a thousand intimate pages addressed to one person without forming some conception, however ideal, of her appearance. Her wit and vivacity are reflected in every letter of Diderot's, and those qualities, in a frail body, seem to imply an appealing countenance, a grace of gesture, and eyes that were not dim behind their glasses. Perhaps this impression is strengthened by one of the few references we find to her in the correspondence of Diderot's friends. Grimm, who was Diderot's most intimate friend, sent her a book (sufficiently philosophical—it was Boulanger's *Recherches sur le despotisme oriental*) and in the accompanying letter he writes:

"Where, Sophie, do you get this passion for philosophy, unknown in persons of your sex and age! How, in the midst of a youth eager for pleasure, when your companions thought only of how to amuse themselves, were you able to ignore or neglect your opportunities so as to devote yourself to meditation and study! If it is true, as Tronchin says, that nature in giving you shape was pleased to lodge the soul of an eagle in a frame of gauze, remember that the first of your duties is to preserve this singular work."

From this and from other evidence M. Babelon concludes that there was a certain intellectual virility in her make-up, and Diderot himself exclaims: "Sophie est homme et femme, quand il lui plaît." But every page belies the image of a forbidding blue-stocking, aggressively clad in whatever were the eighteenth-century equivalents of tweed costumes and low heels. Let each reader picture his Sophie to his own desire. It remains to be added, however, that she was already forty when Diderot met her, some time in 1756; he himself was three years older. Sophie's father, Jean Robert Volland, was a man of some success in public life, who had bought a country estate at Isle-sur-Maine, where he proceeded to build and furnish a château. He had a son who did not survive youth; but his wife and two other daughters play a considerable part in the letters to Sophie, and their personalities become fairly definite to us—more definite, at any rate, than Sophie's own, which is naturally taken so much for granted.

Thirteen years before he met Sophie Diderot had married, in circumstances which promised ill for his future happiness. His wife was the only daughter of a respectable widow who kept a shop for lace and lingerie. Diderot was casually attracted by her face and figure, gained the acquaintance of the family by a subterfuge, wooed the daughter impetuously and only too successfully. In the excitement of the chase he had not hesitated to promise marriage, and Nanette Champion, the lady in question, did not think lightly of her honour. She demanded the fulfilment of his vow, and Diderot, to give him his due, never wavered in his intention. But there were difficulties to be overcome, particularly the objections of Diderot's father; and meanwhile the lovers had become quite disenchanted of each other. But still Nanette persisted in demanding her rights, and in spite of Diderot's warning ("Consider, if I have lost your heart, the greatest danger that you can run is to give me your hand. What makes for happiness in marriage is mutual tenderness") the marriage was accomplished, Diderot escaping for the occasion from the confinement to which his angry father had committed him.

It is not difficult to arrive at a fairly vivid notion of Madame Diderot's character. The main outlines have been given to us by Rousseau in his *Confessions*, in a passage which is too well supported by other evidence to be dismissed as merely due to Rousseau's habitual rancour. Diderot, he wrote:

"had a Nanette just as I had a Thérèse; it was one more similarity between us. But the difference was that my Thérèse, though as good looking as his Nanette, had a sweet temper and a lovable disposition, made to attract a decent fellow; whilst his, a shrew and a scold, in the eyes of others had nothing to compensate for her ill breeding. He married her nevertheless; all very well, if he had made her a promise. As for me, I had done nothing of the sort and was not inclined to follow his example."

Many years later Diderot's daughter, Madame de Vendeul, defended her mother against Rousseau's charges (it was twenty-eight years after his death). She admitted she was a grumbler, but pointed to her gentle birth, her convent education, her beauty and her wisdom. She compared her to a piece of rock-crystal, jagged and unpolished; noble, proud, of a frankness that scorned to hide itself in politeness. Her ignorance of the ways of society, her husband's neglect of her, domestic troubles of all kinds, had embittered her until grumbling had become a habit. "My mother had learned none of the graces which charm the world, but she had a very just and very severe idea of what constitutes good and evil, and, in fact, she esteemed virtue more than she despised vice in the household." It is useless to go into the details of this misalliance; no one can doubt its unhappy reality. Diderot himself, in his letters to Sophie, seems scrupulous to avoid any criticism of his wife. But there is one occasion when the cir-cumstances seem to have been too much for him. In 1762 his wife was ill, and she made a very bad patient. "If an Hospital had two patients like her," Diderot wrote, "it would be necessary to take all the rest away if one wished to preserve them. In her ill humour she has said things to her daughter which cannot be repeated and which kill me. Really, if this child was taken away by some violent illness, I do not know that I should regret it. It is better that she should be dead than left to the mercy of such a mother." Bitterness could not be more terribly expressed, for Diderot loved his daughter; and this outbreak is all the more impressive for its isolated occurrence in the correspondence with Sophie, for to her he naturally divulged all the joys and sorrows to which his mobile spirit was subjected.

It is better to look at the positive side of his emotional life. Such a man was rich in friends. His affectionate relations with Grimm and the Baron d'Holbach, with D'Alembert and his fellow Encyclopædists, are almost unique in literary history. Most remarkable of all, in spite of misunderstandings and even a fantastic quarrel, he maintained the friendship, or shall we say the tolerance, of Rousseau for longer than any of his contemporaries. But now we are concerned with another kind of friendship, again perhaps unique in literary history. The friendship which he formed with Sophie Volland in 1756 lasted without any diminution of fervour until her death in 1784. Naturally a friendship begun at the age of forty and continued until the age of sixty-eight undergoes some mutations—of intensity if not of kind. It is perhaps necessary, therefore, to ask in the first instance what was its actual kind. M. André Billy,* with a directness which we in England can only envy, addresses himself to the question in no uncertain terms, and concludes from various ex-

*Diderot. (Paris: Les Editions de France, 1932.)

pressions and innuendoes in the letters that there can be no possible doubt about it. "Ou les mots n'ont plus de sens, ou l'homme qui a écrit ces lignes était effectivement l'amant de celle qui les a reçues." But do not lovers' thoughts, and accordingly their words, often outrun effectivity; and had we better not conclude in this case, as the late Geoffrey Scott concluded so neatly in the case—a not dissimilar case—of Benjamin Constant and Madame de Charrière, that "psychologically, the character of their relation is abundantly clear; technically, the inquiry would be inconclusive"? ("The subject has its pedantries like any other.") But this technical question apart, the letters abound in passionate declarations; and the sustained intensity of these expressions over so many years may well lead us to reject another sentiment which the author of *The Portrait of Zélide* deduced from the case of Constant and Madame de Charrière. "It may confidently be asserted," wrote Mr. Scott, "that the habit of letter-writing has estranged far more lovers than it has united. It is the devil's device, whereby what seems the bridge of absence becomes the very register of separation. The harmonies of life are one thing; the harmonies of literature another. A literary friendship is a very pretty art in itself; it is a singularly tricky craft if the object be to maintain the sympathies and ascendancies which have been established in the terms of physical contiguity."

There existed in Diderot, as there always exists in men of his temperament, a need for affirmation, for encouragement, for what the Germans call *Bejahung*. Perhaps there comes to such men a suspicion that the judgment of the world, whether it be with them or against them, is anything but firm ground to stand on—that it is no more than an uncertain quicksand of shifting impressions and opinions. They therefore seek for some ideal audience—and it must be an audience of one, to guarantee its integrity and continuity—and to this audience they reveal everything, their hopes and aspirations; and in order that this relationship should not be one-sided, to give it, in fact, its principle of being and growth, it is allied to a mutual passion which will be more or less ideal according to the needs and natures of the participants. In Sophie Diderot found all his needs anticipated. "Sa vie est une attention continue pour moi," he wrote to Grimm; and in his praises of her to other people, as well as in the expression of his passion to Sophie herself, he mingles her moral virtues with her physical charms:

"Ah! Grimm, quelle femme! Comme cela est tendre, doux, honnête, délicat, sensé! Le mal est que je ni sçais quand on seroit heureux. Cela réfléchit, cela aime à réfléchir. Nous n'en sçavons pas plus qu'elle en mœurs, en sentimens, en usages, en une infinité de choses importantes. Nous nous sommes amusés et nous nous amusons encore du projet d'un petit château dont les portes sont petites et les fenêtres très grandes. Cela a son jugement, ses vues, ses idées, son sentiment à soi.

C'est la raison leur, leur vérité, leur bon sens, leur vue qui les mènent; ni le public, ni l'autorité, ni quoi que ce soit ni les subjuge. Elles raisonnent; elles écoutent; elles se défendent; elles ne cédent que quand la place n'est plus tenable."

That was written in 1759. The cynic may doubt the durability of such a virtuous love, but in Diderot's case the values of both virtue and passion if anything increase with the years. In a letter to Sophie written six years later, nine years after their first meeting, we see this virtuous admiration allied to a *tutoiement* rare in those days:

"Chère amie, tu ne sçaurois deviner combien je me prise d'avoir sçu rendre justice à toutes tes qualités; combien tu m'étois chère la première fois que je te le dis; combien tu me l'es devenue davantage depuis ce tems là. C'est que ce n'est point une illusion. Le tems dissipe toutes les illusions, et toutes les passions finissent. Plus je t'ai vue et plus je t'ai aimée. Le tems n'a fait qu'accroître ma tendresse; c'est qu'elle étoit fondée sur des qualités dont j'ai senti la réalité et la valeur, de jour en jour. Ton amant n'a fait que suivre l'exemple de tes amis. Ils ont plus d'amitié et moi plus d'amour pour toi que jamais."

But the course of this true love did not run smooth, though not from any fault of the lovers. They had fallen in love with each other at first sight, and the occasion is now and then referred to in the letters. "Nous étions seuls ce jour-là, tous deux appuyés sur la petite table verte. Je me souviens de ce que je vous disois, de ce que vous me répondites. Oh! l'heureux tems que celui de cette table verte!" The little green table was, of course, in Sophie's mother's house, in the Rue des Vieux Augustins. It was a convenient house for two lovers, for Sophie had a room in an obscure part of it, and this room was actually approached by a secret staircase. Madame Volland evidently thought that philosophy would protect her daughter in such a situation. But one day, three years after their first meeting, Madame Volland surprised the lovers in their eyrie.

"We had been together about an hour [wrote Diderot to Grimm] when we heard some one knock; and would you believe it, *mon ami*, she who knocked was none other than her mother. I will spare you the rest. I don't know what came over the three of us. Sophie and I remained standing; her mother opened a desk, took a paper out of it, and then left. Afterwards, she talked of going down to the country, and this time the child [so Diderot called Sophie at the age of forty-three!] has to go. They drag her there to try and kill her with boredom. What a prospect!"

But at this time Sophie's elder sister, Madame Le Gendre, begins to play a part in the lives of the lovers. Madame Le Gendre was unhappily married to a civil engineer of some means, who thought more of his art collections than of his wife. So Sophie's sister spent a good deal of her time in Paris, with her family. She was beautiful, witty and wise; and she was devoted to Sophie. So much so that Diderot actually became jealous of her. But gradually his tone changes. In fact, it seems that he fell a little in love with the sister too. Uranie, as he called her, became their ally, and seems from the middle of the year 1759 onwards to have been present at their rendezvous whenever she was in Paris. These rendezvous, presumably with the consent of the mother, became regularised; and perhaps that regularity is one explanation of the duration of this friendship; for love, too, must have its discipline. They met at the Rue des Vieux Augustins every Thursday morning and every Sunday, and on Sundays Diderot and Sophie were alone for an hour while Madame Volland and Uranie went to mass. But sometimes for six months in the year Sophie would be at their country house, and it is to these absences that we owe the longest and most interesting of Diderot's letters. But exiled to Isle, Sophie became profoundly unhappy, and nothing shows the real nature of her passion for Diderot (all philosophy apart) than the following description of how Diderot found her in the September of 1759, when, determined to melt the opposition of the mother, he escorted her down to Isle, with all the attentions his cavalier nature was capable of. Diderot was invited to stay on for a few days:

"They fall in with any amusements I suggest [he writes to Grimm]; they invite me to those they arrange. Sometimes Sophie is persuaded to come with us; sometimes she refuses. She passes whole hours in the midst of us, without speaking, her eyes closed, her head inclined on the back of her armchair. If anyone reproaches her for her melancholy, she does not trouble to excuse herself. Should she hear my steps as I approach, she says to her sister: 'Sister, 'tis he.' I come in; she does not move; she is content to smile a little at me and to look at me with eyes in which I see, even in this moment of serenity, the deep intimate sorrow which fills her. If I ask her: 'My friend, what are you thinking of?' she replies: 'I think that you will all be very happy when I am no longer here.' And then she gets up and goes away to a room upstairs to weep with all her strength. Clairet has confided to me that this happens frequently. When she comes back, her eyes are tearful and red, and her sister and I noticing it, express to each other with a look the pain we suffer and the pity she inspires in us. Meanwhile her mother seeks to distract us with questions. When she does not succeed, horses are asked for, and she goes for a ride. Madame Legendre accompanies her, and I remain with Sophie; but these moments when we are alone have no longer any sweetness for her. She is silent, dreams, sighs; she takes my hand and presses it; but if I ask her to lean against me, she says: 'My friend, do not get

197

used to that.' She foresees her end and all she says bears on it."

For Sophie loved her mother, and could not sustain this conflict in loyalties. It is difficult to understand Madame Volland. When Diderot first knew her he described her as a sphinx. "Her soul is sealed with seven seals. She is the woman of the Apocalypse. On her brow is written mystery." In his letters he calls her Morphise. But as the years passed by and Morphise realised the immutability of this passion which absorbed her daughter, her opposition relented. She grows to like Diderot, and he begins to understand her; until there comes a time, some nine years after the scene described above, when Sophie is already fifty-two and Diderot fifty-five and their love has reached some serener sublimation, a time when Diderot begins to address his letters to these three women together, "Mesdames et chères amies." The letters continue in the same terms of intimacy; but there is no longer any reason why this intimacy should not be shared with the two beings who shared everything with Sophie. It was not to be their privilege for long; Madame Le Gendre died this same year, and her mother followed her two years later. But meanwhile Sophie's younger sister, Madame de Blacy, had left a bankrupt husband and rejoined her parents.

As yet we have not touched upon the predominant interest of these letters. Their intimate interest is so strong that we should be glad to possess them for it alone. But Diderot was no ordinary man; he is one of the most complete personalities in the whole range of literary history, abounding in energy, in wit, in knowledge, in every quality which a great man should possess—except, perhaps, reverence. And he had the ability to communicate his entire self to his writing, especially the writing of these letters. The letters to Sophie Volland are, in fact, Diderot's journal, and he himself regarded them in this light. In their course he frequently speaks of them as his journal. "I love," he writes to Sophie, "to live under your eyes. I only remember such moments as I propose to write to you about. All the rest are lost." And everything is poured out, pell-mell: his discussions with D'Holbach and Grimm, his projects for the Encyclopædia, his plans for books, the anecdotes he has heard, the pictures he has seen, the books he has read and so on, down to his indigestions and over-indulgences. "Pour moi, je suis de mon païs," he was fond of saying, and the inhabitants of this "païs" (he was born at Langres, in the province of Marne) "ont beaucoup d'esprit, trop de vivacité, une inconstance de girouettes." This inconstancy he ascribed to the local climate, which changes in twenty-four hours from cold to warm, from calm to stormy, from fair to rainy; and the movements, the ideas, the spirit of the Langrois change with it. In another letter he describes himself more particularly:

"Grimm has told me often that I was made for another world. I don't know if that is true, but

what is certain is that I have been for almost fifty
years a stranger in this one, that I live an imitative
life which is not my own, that I always keep up
with the pace set by others, and that I am like a dog
being taught to walk on two legs. That gives me a
gait sometimes original and sometimes awkward.
What I manage to express is never so good as what
first occurs to me. I speak well only to myself, or
to others when I am not conscious of it. The
quicker I write the better I write. When I happen
to be witty, I am irrepressible. I still don't know of
what I am capable. Fine actions and beautiful
objects move me in the most violent and most
lasting manner. . . . Head in the clouds, I see a
straw on the ground. What I have once admired, I
always admire. I don't bother much with anything
which does not appeal to my heart. . . . Two
tender eyes please me better than the whole
universe."

It is the portrait of a sentimentalist, perhaps, but this
sentimentalist could deal with hard facts, as the
Encyclopædia was to show. And he can work.
Most of all he reminds us of his contemporary
Laurence Sterne. Put Sterne in Diderot's Paris, and
make him a journalist instead of a country parson,
and it would be hard to distinguish the two men. If
the *Journal to Eliza* had been more than a sorry
fragment, Diderot's *Letters to Sophie* might have had
their exact English equivalent. As it is, we find a
closer parallel in Swift's *Journal to Stella*. It is a

different world and a different genius; but the material is very close in its mode of inspiration, its circumstances and its form.

Diderot's zest, his boundless gusto, carries him into every corner of the contemporary scene. His descriptions of the dinners and the country-house parties at the houses of his friends Grimm and D'Holbach cannot be rivalled as pictures of the intimate manners (and what manners!) of the period. But above all this there is such a harvest of incidental interest. In what brilliant and incisive criticism, for example, Sophie is recommended the reading of Hobbes. He advised her to read the *Treatise on Human Nature* three times every year; it is a catechism of which she must not lose a single word. In comparison, Locke is diffuse and careless, La Bruyère and La Rochefoucauld poor and petty. How forcibly, too, Sophie is scolded for not appreciating the virtues of *Pamela!* The amusing anecdote of the trick Lord Chesterfield played on Montesquieu may have been told elsewhere with more circumstance, but not with more wit. The episode of John Wilkes and the Neapolitan courtesan is a farcical masterpiece in miniature, as good as any chapter in *Tristram Shandy*. And there is a long report of the Baron D'Holbach's visit to England in 1765 which is a most interesting comment, full of comic detail. Three things impressed the Baron most forcibly: our predilection for suicide (a pond in St. James's Park being reserved for the exclusive use of women), our lack of sociability, and our missionaries

—a gloomy picture relieved only by our efficient system of stage-coaches and Mr. Garrick's villa on the Thames.

More serious letters give us whole slices from the Encyclopædia (on the religious customs of the Chinese or the theosophic system of the Saracens), but in the end we always return to Sophie. After one such divagation, lasting for some twenty pages, the lover breaks through the Encyclopædist in this transport:

"I have seen all the wisdom of nations and have then thought that it is not worth the sweet folly which my friend inspires in me. I have heard their sublime discourses and have thought that a word from her mouth would fill my soul with an emotion which they do not give. They depict virtue to me and I am persuaded; but I would much rather have seen my friend, looked at her in silence and let fall a tear which her hand would have wiped away or her lips have collected. They try to decry voluptuousness and its intoxication, because it is fleeting and deceptive; yet I burn to find it in the arms of my friend, because there it is renewed whenever she pleases, and because her heart is true and her caresses tender. They tell me: You will age; and I reply to myself: Her years will pass with mine. You will both die, they say; and I add: If my friend dies before me, I shall weep for her, and I shall be happy in weeping. She brings me happiness to-day; to-morrow she will bring me

happiness, and the day after to-morrow, and the
next day, and for ever, because she will not
change, because the gods have given her intelligence, uprightness, sensibility, frankness, virtue,
the truth which never changes. And I close my
ears to the austere counsels of philosophy; *et je fis
bien, n'est-ce pas, ma Sophie?*"

In the end our philosopher must confess that "the
language of the heart is a thousand times more
varied than that of the intelligence, and it is impossible to give the rules of its dialectic." "La
philosophie n'est que l'opium des passions. C'est la
vieillesse d'un moment."

The surviving letters cease in 1774, but there is no
reason to doubt that the friendship lasted until 1784,
the year in which the two lovers died within a
month or two of each other. In her will Sophie left
Diderot "sept volumes des 'Essais' de Montaigne
reliés en maroquin rouge, puis une bague que
j'appelle ma Pauline." It is fitting that their romance
should end on such a precise, such a tender, note.

PABLO PICASSO

PABLO PICASSO was born at Malaga on October 25, 1881. His mother was an Italian, and it is her name that Picasso eventually adopted. His father, Ruiz Blasco, was a drawing-master, and early taught Picasso the rudiments of the art. The family moved from Malaga to Pontevedra, to La Coruña, and finally to Barcelona, where, at the age of fourteen, Picasso entered the School of Fine Arts. But his talent was already prodigious, and there still exist paintings done by him at this age which have all the sureness of a master's hand. After a year at the Barcelona school, Picasso passed to the principal school of art in Spain at Madrid. In 1900 he made his first journey to Paris, and there, in the following year, he held his first exhibition. It was an immediate success. In 1903 he definitely took up his residence in Paris.

Picasso is not the first artist to shuffle out of the skin he was born in; artists in general have been rather prone to change their domicile. But such artists—an El Greco in Spain or a Holbein in England—have usually become in some degree naturalised, and have even, as in the case of El Greco, become exponents of some subtle aspect of the spirit of their adopted countries which hitherto had never been so well felt and expressed. When Picasso left Spain to settle in France, he did not become a Frenchman, but he ceased to be a Spaniard; he became a citizen of the world or, in the sense of that phrase, an artist of the world.

Up to this time, and until 1906, Picasso's work shows a certain consistency. It is usual to distinguish a "Blue Period" lasting until 1904, and a "Rose Period" lasting until 1906, but this is merely a distinction based on the predominant colouring of his paintings, and has no justification in method or form of composition. All his early work is manifestly traditional; that is to say, one can trace in it the influence of the great Spanish masters—Zurbaran, even Velazquez, and certainly Goya (as in the magnificent portrait of the Señora Ricard Canals in the Museum of Catalonian Art, Barcelona); and sometimes mingled with this strain, sometimes separate, the influence of the French Impressionists and Post-impressionists—the influence of Manet and Degas, and above all of Toulouse-Lautrec. The influence of Cézanne is not at first very decisive, but probably Picasso had not seen any of Cézanne's work before he first came to Paris in 1900, and may not have seen it in any quantity until 1903. Over the whole of this period the influence of Toulouse-Lautrec would seem to have been the most decisive. It shows itself above all in a predilection for the same subject-matter—types and genre-subjects from the music-halls, circuses and bars of Barcelona and Paris. Both in colour and composition these paintings betray a psychological emphasis which some critics have not hesitated to call sentimental; and since there is a suggestion that the subsequent development of

Picasso's style is in some sense a mask for this sentimentality, we must ask what such a criticism really implies.

Sentimentality is a desperate word to hurl at an artist of any kind, and nowadays we are all so sensitive about it, that the charge is very liable to produce inhibitions and distortions. We should, therefore, be quite clear what we mean by the word. It always implies some disproportion between an emotion and its cause. It is not suggested, for example, that the emotion of love is in itself sentimental; it only becomes sentimental when an object is unworthy of the kind and degree of love lavished upon it, as in the case of the English love of animals. Such a misapplication of love is due to a defect of judgment, and generally we may say that sentimentality is the display of emotion unchecked by rational judgment. Sentimental art in this sense is art which arouses these unchecked emotions, either directly or by association. Certainly some of Picasso's early pictures, those, for example, of blind men, and a well-known one, in the Chicago Art Institute, of an "Old Guitarist," come within range of this charge. The point to determine in any such case is, first, the validity of the emotion expressed, and, secondly, the æsthetic worth of the expression. If the æsthetic worth is *nil*, the question need not be discussed. If the æsthetic worth is considerable, as in the case of the "Old Guitarist," then the only question is to what degree does the sentiment of the picture interfere with our æsthetic enjoyment? And that is probably a question for the individual; the normal person, I think, can stand a good deal of irrelevant sentiment, and even downright sentimentality, if the design and colour of the picture are of sufficient interest. But actually the question is more often than not automatically cancelled; for the great artist tends to become so absorbed in the purely æsthetic meaning of his picture, that he grows jealous of this subsidiary psychological interest, and gradually excludes it. This may not be true of all periods of art, but it is certainly true of modern art. Picasso, in this respect, merely repeats the development of Turner, Cézanne, or Matisse. Only the change, in his case, has a somewhat apocalyptic suddenness.

The years 1906–7 are sometimes called his "Negro Period," and here and there, in the paintings and drawings of this time, one can trace the influence, more or less direct, of Negro sculpture, the artistic qualities of which were then becoming recognised. But such influences are completely absorbed in the general tendency towards abstraction of which Picasso was henceforth to be the leader. In a large canvas always discussed in books about Picasso, "Les Demoiselles d'Avignon," *tableau capital de l'œuvre de Picasso*, painted in 1906–7, we have a broad flat design made up of five nudes and their fluttering draperies. The lines of their bodies and the folds of the draperies are angularised; the background and shadows are intensified to emphasise this geometric effect; the faces of the young ladies are a rather incongruous assembly of Negro masks. Apart from these masks, there is a complete disappearance of what I have called a psychological appeal, and even in the masks that appeal is disintegrating. The subject is meant to shock rather than to attract. But such a picture is only a transitional piece; more significant, for the future, are a series of still-lifes painted during 1907 and 1908, in which we see a patient simplification of the forms, tending towards an almost complete geometricisation. In 1909 the process was applied to the human form. The logical end of this process was complete abstraction, and this logic Picasso accepted.

The process was, of course, inherent in the practice of Cézanne, who had conceived the art of painting as the art of giving permanence and solidity to the evanescent impressions of visual experience. Instead of catching the shimmering surface of appearances, the momentary effects of light and movement, Cézanne sought to reveal a permanent reality, to feel nature as eternal, and in this attempt he arrived, almost unconsciously, at something like a geometricisation of objects; nature, he said, could be resolved into the cylinder, the sphere, and the cone. But that effect, with Cézanne, was a by-product of his primary aim, which was still to realise his sensations in the face of natural phenomena. Picasso, though he may have begun with a similar aim, and though some of his early cubist paintings succeed exactly as Cézanne's succeeded, carried the process a stage farther. He found that the cylinder, the sphere, and the cone were satisfactory objects in themselves, and that out of such elements he could construct a design which conveyed all the purely æsthetic appeal inherent in any painting.

Though such a literal interpretation was novel, actually the theory which justifies such a step had been current for some time. Without, on this occasion, referring to its presence in Plato,* let me quote a paragraph from an essay written in England in 1877:

"Art, then, is thus always striving to be independent of the mere intelligence, to become a matter of pure perception, to get rid of its responsibilities to its subject or material; the ideal examples of poetry and painting being those in which the constituent elements of the composition are so welded together, that the material or subject no longer strikes the intellect only; nor the form, the eye or the ear only; but form and matter, in their union or identity, present one single effect to the 'imaginative reason,' that complex faculty for which every thought and feeling is twin-born with its sensible analogue or symbol."

Pater, from whose essay on "The School of Giorgione" this passage comes, has been so persistently misrepresented and misunderstood, that perhaps it is a mistake to resuscitate his theory, with all its melancholy aftermath of "art for art's sake." One does so in justice to Pater, and because his expression of the theory is not likely to be bettered. It is true that

*Cf. Art Now, pp. 101-3.

events since Pater's time have given a very different complexion to the theory, and probably he would not countenance the application we are now making. But theories, when they are logically incontrovertible, have the power of running away from their authors, and reaping whatever comes into their path. At the end of many centuries of critical consideration, and in virtue of a vast amount of accumulated wisdom, there seems no avoiding the conclusion, that if we are to keep our æsthetic judgments, whether in poetry, painting, or music, clear of all irrelevant facts, then those judgments must be based on the operative sensibilities, and on those sensibilities alone. No criticism that is not a criticism of form in its relation to matter has ever advanced any of the arts a single step. The virtue of any art wholly inheres in its appeal to the senses and the "imaginative reason," and all other criteria, whether moral or sociological, are *æsthetically* irrelevant. It is criticism of a wider scope and a different kind that attempts to relate æsthetic values to their social environment—to explain the distortions which these values suffer in the historical circumstances of a particular period, and in the estimation of all succeeding periods. It is sometimes necessary, however, to maintain the autonomy of art, as of philosophy, however abstract and theoretical such an attitude may sometimes seem.

Such a distinction does not rest on the narrow basis of modern art. Any coherent conception of art extending beyond the Renaissance in Europe, and open to the appeal of Byzantine art, of Oriental art, of African art, of Palæolithic art—indeed, of art wherever and whenever it issues from the clear perceptions and instinctive expressions of man, is based on æsthetic sensibility, and not on historical objectivity. Admittedly the word sensibility, in this context, includes such "intellectual" reactions as are involved in the apprehension of formal relations; and art is a dialectical process which holds in suspense such "identical opposites" as idealism and materialism, individuality and universality, romantic and classic—the whole logic of its intensity depending on such a resolution of conflicting elements.

It was necessary to make this protest because there is a persistent attempt to associate an artist like Picasso with doctrines that inflame the political passions of deans and moneylenders; the fact being that no one is more oblivious of those doctrines than an artist like Picasso. The art of Picasso has no implications outside the studio; it is as non-significant as the music of Bach or Mozart; as pure as the poetry of Racine or Mallarmé.* It is wholly concentrated, to quote Pater again, in "that inventive or creative handling of pure line and colour which . . . is quite independent of anything definitely poetical in the subject it accompanies."

*I have expressed a somewhat different view in a pamphlet written more recently than this essay (*Essential Communism.* Stanley Nott, Ltd., 1935). If one is to take into account such wide sociological generalisations as, for example, "the disintegration of the bourgeois concept of reality," then undoubtedly the art of Picasso has a significance beyond the studio. In that sense Bach and Mozart express their *Zeitgeist.* But there is a considerable difference between a *Zeitgeist* and the dogmas of a particular sect or party. I hope to treat this question much more adequately in one of my next books.

Picasso's aim has always been to extend the material of the artist, to overcome the limitations of the normal equipment of the painter. From 1913 to 1915 he experimented in *papiers collés*, that is to say, in designs made up of coloured and printed papers, gummed on to a canvas or board, sometimes completed with details in oil or pencil. On the basis of these experiments we then have a series of paintings which create designs of a much more complicated structure and more varied texture. These were painted intermittently with a series of so-called neo-classic pictures, in which Picasso returns to a figurative or representational mode of painting, with classical themes as his subject-matter. Especially in the form of drawings and etchings, these exercises are strongly reminiscent of Greek vase paintings, or the engraved designs on Greek and Etruscan mirror-backs. Occasionally the themes are modern, as in the portraits of his wife and child, and in the drawings of his friends and contemporaries, such as Stravinsky and Ansermet.

About 1925 Picasso began to paint a new type of abstraction, which calls for an entirely new theory of explanation. Such a theory is only offered to those who need an intelligent excuse for their æsthetic perceptions. Æsthetically, there is no difference between any of the forms art assumes, as Picasso himself has said. The only important distinction is that between nature and art, and once that distinction has been made, on the evidence of all art whatsoever, then the only difference between one form of art and another is the degree of conviction which it carries. "From the point of view of art, there are no concrete or abstract forms, but only forms which are more or less convincing lies. That these lies are necessary for our spiritual being is beyond any doubt, because with them we form our æsthetic image of the world."

This statement is taken from an interview which Picasso gave to a German art critic, Paul Westheim. The book in which it was published (*Künstlerbekenntnisse:* Berlin, Propyläen Verlag) bears no date, but from internal evidence it would seem that the interview was given before 1925, that is to say, before the decisive change in Picasso's style already mentioned took place. But in this interview there is another statement of great psychological interest, which seems almost to anticipate the new style. Picasso says he cannot understand why so much importance is attached to the word "research" in modern painting. Painting has nothing to do with seeking, but is concerned only with finding. "Among the many sins charged against me, none has less justification than that which says the spirit of research is the most important element in my work. When I paint, I set about to indicate what I have found, and not what I am seeking. In art, to will is not enough. As we say in Spain: Love is proved by deeds, not by arguments. What a man does is all that counts, not what he intends to do.

"We all know that art is not truth. Art is a fiction that enables us to recognise the truth—at least, such truth as is given to us to understand. The artist must know the ways and means of convincing others of the truthfulness of his fictions. When his art only indicates that he has sought or investigated the best means of persuading other people to accept his fictions, then nothing is achieved.

"The idea of investigation has often led painting into error and forced the artist into fruitless lucubrations. This is perhaps the main fault of modern art. The spirit of inquiry has poisoned all those who do not fully grasp the positive and fundamental elements of modern art, for it has led them to wish to paint the invisible and therefore the unpaintable."

At first this statement seems to be a complete denial of Picasso's practice during the last nine years. But all depends on what he means by the act of seeing. We see outwardly and represent the apparent nature of things; and we see inwardly and represent the world of the imagination. The mistake is to think, in the manner of the Impressionists, that there exists a more exact or more scientific mode of vision, which it is the business of the artist to exploit. Picasso's meaning is made quite clear from a later statement, reported by M. Zervos in *Cahiers d'Art*, 1932. "*Je vois pour les autres*," that is to say, as an artist he sees things which other people cannot see—he has visions, as we say, "*apparitions soudaines qui s'imposent à moi*." He does not know in advance what he is going to put on the canvas, nor does he decide what colours to use. He does not will to do anything, he does not seek to do anything. He allows his sensibilities a free rein, paints in a trance—a trance which has all the acuteness, the visual definiteness of dreams. His only care is to be faithful to what is given, to what is found, to paint what he sees.

Those who are familiar with the paintings done by Picasso in this latest phase of his career will find any verbal description of them very inadequate, but in the absence of illustrations I must make some attempt to differentiate them from the normal type of abstract painting. The normal conception of an abstract picture is comparatively simple: it is the disposition, on a plane surface, of lines and colours in an æsthetically pleasing pattern. Logically, no further definition is necessary. The pattern may have some more or less remote relation to objects, but such a relationship is not necessary. The painting, like an eastern carpet, is a decorative design within a rectangular frame. As such it is completely justified as decorative art, but art gains an additional force if it expresses a subjective reaction to the objects of perception—if the artist adopts, as it were, an attitude of intellectual love towards the world of his creation. The transition from the decorative to the creative is not easy to explain in general terms: in Picasso's case it involves a renunciation of the will and a surrender to the promptings of the unconscious, which promptings, far from being decorative, are presumably symbolic.

The later pictures of Picasso differ from his pure abstractions in that they do definitely represent "something." This something is often a strangely distorted female form; heads incomprehensibly interlocked or dislocated; swollen forms in which one can still distinguish a stretched mouth, an occluded eye; vague rhythmical shapes which can still be identified as a monstrous bust, a branch of leaves, a bowl of fruit, a guitar; gigantic sculptural figures built up with misshapen bones, or of bones with some complex function, like the bones of the ear; forms fœtal and nightmarish, actual and vital. The colours in these compositions are clear and strident; the composition usually simple and architectural. More recently, as if not satisfied with the limitations of paint and canvas, Picasso has begun to model such conceptions in plaster, to cast them in bronze, to construct them in metals and any materials at hand.

Such works of art cannot be rationally explained without some theory of the unconscious origin of imagery. In the state in which he admittedly paints these pictures, Picasso is obviously in the condition of day-dreaming, perhaps a condition of self-hypnosis. Apart from any æsthetic considerations, the value of such art will depend on the significance of the imagery which he brings to the surface and transfers directly to his canvas. What can be affirmed, on the evidence of many people who have seen such paintings, is that their imagery has a very haunting quality. Whatever the nature of the vitality expressed by Picasso, it has an undoubted power of fascination. I do not think the purely æsthetic qualities in the paintings—their colour harmonies and formal arrangement—can be dismissed as unimportant in the total effect. Picasso is too essentially an artist ever to betray his innate talent for form and colour, and I should say that this talent is all the surer for being exercised under purely instinctive conditions.

The important qualification to make about such art—for Picasso's example in this respect as in all others has been quickly followed by a host of imitators—is that it should be involuntary. To will is not enough. Conscious research is fatal. The artist must paint what he finds; he must not seek for something he has not found. Not many artists are capable of observing those conditions; for they are the conditions of the rarest form of inspiration. "The Genius of Poetry," wrote Keats, "must work out its own salvation in a man. It cannot be matured by law and precept, but by sensation and watchfulness in itself. That which is creative must create itself." That is true of all the arts, and Picasso, more abundantly than any of his contemporaries, has been creative, even to the extent of creating the art he practises.

Though he has extended the possible world of art, and brought within its scope material that was never thought of before, yet it is important to remember that Picasso retains all his previous conquests. The idea of an evolution in Picasso's art is, as he has declared, quite foreign to its nature. Extension is more than development. Everything Picasso creates comes from the same centre, a vital genius for all modes of plastic expression; even when, in the midst of painting the spectres of his unconscious intuition, he turns aside and makes a drawing which in grace and sensibility and objective truth not Ingres nor Raphael could excel. Every mode of expression is valid, and each is the man, who is to be accepted in all the fullness and complexity of his genius.

PARALLELS
IN ENGLISH PAINTING
AND POETRY

ALTHOUGH we use the word "artist" in a narrow sense, to mean a painter or a sculptor, properly speaking it includes everyone who brings skill to the making of an object. Some of the arts, such as the art of the potter or the art of the cook, are regarded as minor arts; others are put on a higher plane and called fine arts. Actually it is very difficult to draw a hard-and-fast line between the minor arts and the fine arts; between the art of the builder, for example, and the art of the architect. The unknown builder of a cottage in the Cotswolds may be a better artist than the architect of a palatial bank in London. In the end we have to give up all attempts to arrange the arts in order of importance. Some people have argued that we must give up all attempts even to compare one art with another; each art, they say, has its own laws, its own history and development, and criticism should not confuse them. Each art, in other words, has its own tradition, and though a painter may learn from the great painters of the past —from Giotto and Raphael and Michelangelo, from Rubens and Rembrandt—he will, if he is a wise man, not trouble about Homer or Dante or Shakespeare. They will only put wrong ideas into his head.

In spite of the force of such an argument, I think there is still a sense in which all arts are art, and the higher we go in the scale of the arts, the more they have in common. In this essay I am going to take

225

two of the highest of the arts—the arts of painting and poetry—and see if it is possible to trace, in our own country, certain parallels in their development. Both arts have their roots in the same soil; they suffer the same historical fate, the same economic and social conditions, even the same climate. Surely this wide community of circumstance must result in some common features! And if we find, in any given period, wide differences between the level of achievement in the two arts—if the same conditions give rise to different results—then that too will be a subject worth investigation.

Our first difficulty will be to find a common starting point. In painting it is comparatively simple. The rise of the great school of manuscript illumination at Winchester in the tenth century marks a definitely English stage in the history of art. The Winchester style, as we call it, has relations with the earlier Celtic style, and it has affinities with the contemporary Carolingian style. Nevertheless, it is English in certain distinct characteristics, and these characteristics are henceforth to persist in the development of our painting. But what can we call English in the poetry of the tenth century? There is, of course, a fragmentary but artistically important body of Anglo-Saxon poetry, and there are outstanding works like *Beowulf*, which I believe is usually dated about the beginning of the eighth century, and there is the *Seafarer*, which belongs to the tenth century. But if we are to make any comparison between the poetry and the painting of this age, we are immediately faced with a difficulty which arises from a fundamental difference in the two arts. The painting of the tenth century can speak to us to-day as directly as it spoke to the Anglo-Saxons ten centuries ago; but their poetry is cloaked in a dead language. It is true that we can, at the cost of a good deal of trouble, learn this language, and it has sufficient affinities with modern English, perhaps, to enable us to appreciate some of the overtones of its poetic appeal. But poetry is embedded in language, and its history is dependent on the history of language. Painting, on the other hand, exploits unchanging materials—line, colour and form—and is therefore timeless and international in its appeal. The changes which take place in the subject-matter of painting—in its spiritual content, let us say—do naturally modify its appeal, or the nature of the reaction it provokes. We must make some allowance for the difference between the psychology of a tenth-century monk and that of a sophisticated art-lover of the present day. But such an allowance must be made for poetry also, so this consideration does not affect our comparison.

I do not feel that much value would survive in a comparison of a translation from the Anglo-Saxon and a manuscript of the same period, such as the Benedictional of St. Aethelwold, which illustrates very well the characteristics of the Winchester School of illumination towards the end of the tenth century: a linear grace beneath which we still discern something of the geometrical angularity of the preceding Celtic style, a certain sombreness of feeling combined with a richness of colouring. These are very general characteristics, but if we descend to greater detail we shall, especially in this early period, become aware of another technical difference between the two arts which makes comparison difficult. Painting is an objective art, expressed in a fixed material form; it is often portable, and carries with it wherever it goes, and so long as it survives, the characteristics the artist gave it. This means that various elements of style, originating at different periods and in different places, may be found in one place at some particular time; and any one work of plastic art, at a sufficiently advanced stage in the history of a civilisation, may borrow elements from any centre within that civilisation. Thus, an Anglo-Saxon manuscript illumination has elements derived from Celtic, Carolingian, Italo-Byzantine and even ancient Greek sources. *Literature*, on the other hand, being more often a subjective mode of expression, coming straight from the heart, as we say, is dependent on nothing more objective than the form of the language used by a particular person at a particular time. It is infinitely more direct and single in its scope. It is a more spontaneous art.

The spontaneous origin of poetry is well illustrated by the story of the poet Caedmon as told by the Venerable Bede. "This man," Bede tells us, "had lived a secular life till he had reached old age, and had never learned a song. And so often at the feast, when it was decreed for the sake of mirth that each in turn should sing to the harp, when he saw the harp coming near him, then in shame he rose from the banquet, and went home to his house. One time when he had done this, and had left the house where the feasting was, and had gone out to the cattle-stall, for the care of them was entrusted to him that night, and had duly laid his limbs to rest there and fallen asleep, there appeared a man unto him and hailed him and saluted him and called him by his name: Caedmon, sing me something. Then he answered and said: I cannot sing, and so I left the feasting and came hither because I could not. He who spoke to him again said: Nevertheless, thou canst sing to me. He said: What am I to sing? He said: Sing me the Creation. When he received that answer, then straightway he began to sing in praise of God, the Creator, verses and words which he had never heard before." This parable illustrates what I mean by the comparative spontaneity of poetry. The plastic arts are by comparison full of derivative elements—made up of details of style and conventions of handling which have very diverse antecedents in the history of art. Students of Anglo-Saxon literature will no doubt be ready to contend that there are technical elements in the poetry which are also of historical derivation. The metre of Anglo-Saxon verse, for example, is of a rigid pattern and retains this pattern for centuries. But this very uniformity of the verse-form really supports my contention, for against the technical uniformity of the poetry we must put the technical diversity of the drawing and painting. To effect a direct comparison between the graphic and the poetic arts of the period, we must try to separate out in each art an element which is peculiar to the period, or at least particularly significant. In the illuminations it is not difficult to fix on their linear quality as just such an element. Deriving from the earlier Celtic style (perhaps through the intermediary of the Carolingian school) there is, in the Anglo-Saxon style of drawing, not only an emphasis on outline, but a free play with such outline often amounting to a tendency towards geometrical abstraction, a love of line for the sake of the abstract patterns it makes. If we then ask ourselves what is the most significant stylistic element in Anglo-Saxon verse, we shall have no hesitation in answering: the elaborate use of alliteration. The whole structure of Anglo-Saxon verse is built up on a system of alliterative metre. Here, perhaps, my thesis becomes fanciful, but I wish to suggest that the same spirit which expressed itself in linear emphasis in the case of drawing, when it came to verse expressed itself in alliteration. Alliteration is a horizontal movement across the structure of the verse; it is linear abstraction within verbal expression. In a corresponding way, the play of lines in a drawing will show a continual repetition of the same motive, a kind of linear alliteration.

That, I think, is the first significant parallel which it is possible to find in the history of our art and literature. Its validity as a comparison will perhaps be more evident if we can find similar parallels at other periods.

230

The Conquest imposed upon England a foreign culture, and French became the language of the court, but I do not think that there occurred in the culture of the country any such catastrophic break as our school histories would lead us to suppose. Naturally there came over with the Norman court, Norman artists and Norman poets, and the culture of the court was predominantly French; in the course of two or three centuries this culture was gradually absorbed by the background or native culture, producing first Chaucer, then Spenser, and finally the perfect English amalgam of the Elizabethan drama. But in spite of the Conquest, the Anglo-Saxon tradition in our art and literature persisted among the great body of the people, and among the people I include the clerks and craftsmen who were mainly responsible for the popular art and literature of the twelfth and thirteenth centuries. It is true that during this period there were written a certain number of chronicles and romances which are French in origin and feeling; and these are the works which bulk large in our literary histories. It may be equally true that some of the cathedrals of the time were designed and their erection supervised by French architects. But in the case of poetry there is no reason to suppose that the succession of ballad-singers and reciters, who maintained the real traditions of our literature, was ever interrupted by the Conquest; whereas in the world of art, whether it is architecture, illumination, ivory and metal work, or enamelling, there is the clearest evidence for the persistence of an unbroken tradition from Anglo-Saxon times. Naturally there is a development of style due to the slow changes in sentiment and feeling which take place over any period of time, but in typical post-Conquest works such as the Bury St. Edmunds Bible (1121-1148), the Psalter of Westminster Abbey, and above all in the great Winchester Bible of about 1160-70, the persistence of the Anglo-Saxon tradition and style is perfectly evident. The same facts may be observed in the wall-paintings and stained glass of the period.

The literature of the period that I shall take as truly representative is found in the ballads and popular religious poetry. Such poetry in most cases only reaches us in a traditional form—that is to say, although it originated in the twelfth or thirteenth century, it was handed down orally for several generations, and only received the final form in which we know it as late as the fifteenth or sixteenth century or even later. Perversions and even transmutations of the original poems undoubtedly took place, but we know that the essential features were preserved. To take as an example the well-known ballad of *Hugh of Lincoln:* the legend on which this ballad is based goes back to the thirteenth century, though the first written record of it is as recent as the middle of the eighteenth century. But through centuries of oral tradition it has preserved its original characteristics. These characteristics are: First, a clean directness of narrative. No time is lost on details which serve no purpose in forwarding the action; there is no comment, no criticism, no probing into motives. Secondly, we notice a certain fierce realism, which a more squeamish age would call callous and inhuman. It is, of course, nothing of the sort. If you want to be callous you should be pathological; you should work on the nerves of the reader. But crude slaughter-house butchery, such as delights children in the tale of *Jack the Giantkiller*, or of *Bluebeard*, has the effect of phantasy. It may thrill, but it does not sicken or excruciate. I would not like to give the impression, however, that what I call realism in the ballads is confined to bloody acts. An observation like:

> *He kicked the ba' with his right foot,*
> *And catch'd it wi' his knee*

which comes from *Hugh of Lincoln*, is every bit as realistic as:

> *She's laid him on a dressing-table*
> *And stickit him like a swine*

from the same ballad. What in the jargon of literary criticism we call realism is no more than definiteness. To the directness of the narrative corresponds a definiteness of visualisation, and this definiteness is the most characteristic feature of the ballads.

The technical device of alliteration, though some-what more loosely applied, persists throughout medieval English poetry, and a new device, the refrain, repeated at the end of each verse, becomes very popular. The refrain is often quite meaningless, at any rate in the form in which it reaches us, and perhaps its significance is musical rather than literary; in the repetition of the ballads it was perhaps sung as a chorus by the listeners. Any parallel in the plastic arts would be far-fetched. But before passing on to the plastic arts, we should notice that in its content the ballad poetry, and the contemporary lyrical poetry, continues to express the pessimism prevalent in Anglo-Saxon poetry. It does not seem that this mood of pessimism was induced by Christianity; the carols and the poems which celebrate Christ's nativity are cheerful interludes in the general despondency, though on the other hand there is no doubt that in the doctrine of original sin Christianity had given the inherent pessimism of the northern races a motive or symbol round which they could weave their gloomiest fancies. So characteristic is this gloom of northern peoples in general, that we must assume, I think, that it was determined by their bitter struggle against the hostile forces of nature. That environing hostility made men not only hardy and courageous in action, but also superstitious and gloomy in belief. The elements they faced were endowed with supernatural attributes, and were only to be exorcised by magic rites. Christianity did little to enliven the prevailing gloom; it seemed rather to complete the spiritual condition of the northern races, expanding just those aspects of belief most evident to them—the state of original sin, the transitoriness of earthly joys, the reality of the supernatural world. The art of such a spiritual condition is an art of escape; but though it is an art of escape, it is not an art of deceit or self-deception. Just as in the corresponding plastic and graphic arts the tendency is towards an abstraction which nevertheless is always based on, or returns to, the living forms of animals and plants, so in this verbal art of poetry the tendency all the time is to seek the abstraction of alliteration and the refrain, but always to ally it with the vitality and vivacity of an eager sensibility.

The works of art of the twelfth and thirteenth centuries are sufficiently numerous to make any selection arbitrary, but I defy anyone to find anything particularly cheerful in the art of the period. Apart from a preoccupation with gloomy subjects, such as the Harrowing of Hell and the Last Judgment, there is, in the depiction of such comparatively joyful subjects as the Nativity and the Entry into Jerusalem, a solemnity and realism altogether inappropriate to the scenes. And this characteristic of our early Gothic art is something quite distinct from the hieratic solemnity of Byzantine art. There is, I should say, about the same difference between the two, as there is between a medieval Latin poem like *Dies Irae* and that grim cradle-song from the Kildare manuscript, the last verse of which reads:

> *Child, thou nert a pilgrim,*
> *Bot an uncuthe gist;*
> *Thi dayés beth itold;*
> *Thi iurneis beth icast.*

Whoder thou salt wend,
North other est,
Deth the sal betide,
With bitter bale in brest.
Lollai, lollai, litil child!
This wo Adam the wroght,
Whan he of the appil ete,
And Eve hit him betacht.

Whatever examples we take from the plastic arts of the period, manuscripts like the Psalter of St. Swithin's Priory or sculpture such as that at Malmesbury, they show clearly that those qualities which we found characteristic of the popular poetry of the early Gothic period—briefly, directness of narrative, realism of presentation, and pessimism of content, are equally discernible in the plastic arts of the period; and still I do not think it is too fanciful to relate certain technical processes in both kinds of art, since in each case these processes show a tendency towards abstraction and away from naturalism which is perhaps a reflex of the prevailing spiritual pessimism.

That pessimism reached a kind of delirium in the Black Death of 1348–9, and after that appalling disaster, there was a slow renaissance which brought with it a happier conception of life. That renaissance is typified in poetry by Geoffrey Chaucer, who was a boy at the time of the Black Death, and who died in 1400. The characteristics of Chaucer's poetry are too well known to make it necessary for me to say anything about them here; the only aspect I wish to

236

emphasise is the reconciliation he effected between the aristocratic and the popular elements in our culture. By adopting the vernacular, by proving that English was a language adequate to the general standards of European poetry, he did for English poetry what no one was ever to do for English art. From Chaucer to Spenser and onwards to the Elizabethans and beyond the Elizabethans, the development of English literature is single, independent and fully national; it is a plant with roots in a new and rich soil. The course of art is in no way comparable. It is true that even before the Black Death, at the beginning of the fourteenth century, a new humanism had begun to make itself apparent in the plastic arts, and English art, always inclined to elegance, was turning to sweetness and even to sentimentality or prettiness. There is a well-known wall-painting at Chichester, a roundel of the Virgin and Child of about 1260, which already has traces of this quality. The Wilton Diptych might be quoted as a work of art contemporary with Chaucer, and quite Chaucerian in feeling, but as there is no agreement that this work is English, I must not press the comparison. In the illuminated manuscripts of the period, the same humanising, naturalising tendency goes on apace, often helped by foreign influences, Flemish and Bohemian and Burgundian—and by the time we reach the first half of the fifteenth century, in a manuscript such as the Bedford Book of Hours, all the qualities typical of the early manuscripts have entirely disappeared. The prevailing

sentiment has now more in common with Fra
Angelico or St. Francis than with any native tradition.

The fifteenth century saw the rise of a prosperous
merchant class in England, and many a parish
church, especially in the eastern counties, has
native works of art comparable to the poetry of
Langland or the Miracle Plays, sometimes decorative
and charming, sometimes vigorous and amusing.
But we have only to think of what was happening
in Italy at the same time to gain a due sense of
proportion. For literature we need have no regrets;
it was the fair seed time of our greatest age of poetry,
and the harvest at the end of the sixteenth and
beginning of the seventeenth century was to have no
parallel in the history of European literature. But the
fate of our plastic arts was to be far different, and
between the beginning of the fifteenth century and
the beginning of the eighteenth there is really little to
record that is not secondary in interest or derivative
in style. For an explanation we are driven back to
essential differences in the arts. Poetry is firmly
anchored to the language of a country, and must find
expression within those narrow limits or not at all:
painting and the other plastic arts speak an international language, and therefore we are not so
dependent on a national expression, and can import
our art along with other fashionable goods. With
kings and courts to set such fashions, the current is
soon set against native talent. That the English
artists failed to keep in the fashion is obvious, but it
was also inevitable. As I show in the next essay, the

technical quest which began in Italy with Giotto and Masaccio simply could not enter into the plastic consciousness of the English artist. The source of our technical inspiration had failed in its depths; we had depended so long on a linear mode of expression, that our artists simply could not compete with the new Italian and Flemish methods. It is very interesting to note how during the fifteenth and sixteenth centuries the English tendency towards linear and two-dimensional design persists side by side with the invading chiaroscuro. We find Nicholas Hilliard, the famous miniaturist who was at the beginning of his career at the time of Holbein's first visit to England, affirming that "the principal parts of Painting or Drawing after the life consisteth in truth of line," and "the line without shadowe showeth all to good judgement, but the shadowe without line showeth nothing."

During the Elizabethan period, in which English poetry soared to its dizziest heights, we must abandon any attempt to find our parallels: they simply do not exist. The same is true of the seventeenth century, though here, I think, an interesting parallel might be drawn between poetry and another art, architecture. Dryden and Wren were almost exact contemporaries, and how steadily they both reflect the spirit of their age. Wren's ambition, to build "after a good Roman manner," is a fair enough description of Dryden's ambition in verse. Both built well, according to the best science and taste of their period; both display the same kind of technical ingenuity, the same grace of design and the same richness of decoration. Each, in his particular art, brings the English genius as near as it has ever come to the classical ideal.

In the next century, by enlarging our conception of poetry, it might be possible to draw some parallel between Hogarth and the first great English novelists —Richardson, Fielding and Smollett. Again we are dealing with almost exact contemporaries, and it is surely very significant that the rebirth of English painting should correspond so precisely with the birth of the English novel. Both arts represent a reaction from the stilted classicism of the preceding century, and both represent a return to some of the qualities of medieval art—a love of the grotesque, for example, and a certain realistic violence. But though this comparison is so rich in significance, I must leave it on one side to make way for others more within my present design.

The great parallel towards which we are moving is, of course, that of the Romantic movement at the end of the eighteenth century. That movement, which superficially has all the sudden splendour of a literary revolution, was in fact the final phase of a slow evolution of sentiment. The poetry of Blake, Wordsworth and Coleridge does, of course, in a very real sense represent a reaction "caused by a weariness of artificial and conventional poetry"; it does go back, in order to draw new life into poetry, "to simple human nature, and to Nature herself as seen in her wild and uncultivated beauty." But it would be a mistake to think that the poets of the preceding age had been indifferent to human nature, or Nature herself. They merely treated the subject in a different manner, and that manner, like all manners, only changed slowly. We have already seen that in the early Gothic period our poets and artists tended to distrust nature, and to get away from her in their works. Then came that slow penetration of humanism into the north, which culminated in the classicism of the seventeenth century; and classicism, it should be remembered, by no means ignores nature. It rather tames it and trims it, and makes it thoroughly subordinate to human needs and civilised tastes. When, in England, the seventeenth century closes with Dryden, it is on a note of perfect accord between man and nature. Nature had been tamed and trimmed and framed within a regular perspective, and as such it made an admirable backcloth for the stage of human life. The use of it has, it is true, become very perfunctory by the time we reach Alexander Pope, but Pope is not the only poet of his period, and is not so representative as he is often assumed to be. The more one studies the minor poetry of the eighteenth century, the more conscious one becomes of the gradual growth of a general state of sensibility, which merely culminated in Words- worth. The backcloth is moved forward, and painted in livelier colours. The result is called "picturesque," and once more painting and poetry have a terminology in common. Once more we can draw exact parallels.

241

In poetry the first signs of this new sensibility appear in the *Winter* of James Thomson, published in 1726. Gainsborough was not born till the next year, but Richard Wilson was then twelve years old (Thomson was only twenty-six). After Thomson, in poetry, come Collins, Gray and Goldsmith, not to mention a considerable number of minor poets, all of whom contribute to a slow change of sentiment. In painting, Wilson is followed by Gainsborough, Paul Sandby and Francis Towne. Wilson imported his picturesque conception of landscape from abroad, from Rome, where a school of landscape had existed for a whole century previously. But the developed style of Wilson, especially when he was painting for his own pleasure rather than for a patron's, does show a certain freshness of conception and technique. It is a change quite comparable to that introduced into poetry by Thomson, who deliberately abandoned the rhymed couplet of Pope for the more natural freedom of blank verse. How exactly these lines from Thomson's *Spring* reflect the pictorial conventions of Wilson's landscapes:

See, where the winding vale its lavish stores,
Irriguous, spreads. See, how the lily drinks
The latent rill, scarce oozing through the grass,
Of growth luxuriant; or the humid bank,
In fair profusion, decks. Long let us walk,
Where the breeze blows from yon extended field
Of blossom'd beans. Arabia cannot boast
A fuller gale of joy, than, liberal, thence

Breathes through the sense, and takes the ravished soul.
Nor is the mead unworthy of thy foot,
Full of fresh verdure, and unnumber'd flowers,
The negligence of Nature, wide, and wild;
Where, undisguised by mimic Art, she spreads
Unbounded beauty to the roving eye.

Gainsborough's own preference for his landscapes is a well-established fact, and though we are still far from the direct naturalism of Constable, though the aim is still at all costs a picturesque arrangement rather than a direct transcript, yet so great was Gainsborough's feeling for natural effects, so deft his brushwork and so delicate and fresh his colour, that he evokes completely the atmosphere of the English landscape. It is by a similar magic that Collins and Gray depict the same landscape in their verses. An early landscape of Gainsborough's matches the unrhymed rhythms of Collins's *Ode to Evening*, whilst the still freer and more naturalistic treatment of Gainsborough's later landscapes approaches to the poetic objectivity of Wordsworth.

I come now to what is perhaps the most striking parallel of all—that between Constable and Wordsworth. It is all the more striking since the poet and the painter in this comparison seem to have been totally unaware of each other's achievement. Whilst Constable was carrying out the same revolution in the technique of painting that Wordsworth was carrying out in poetic technique, Wordsworth himself was whole-heartedly admiring the pictures of his friend Sir George Beaumont, a typical representative of the academic conventions of the eighteenth century. And whilst Constable was not unappreciative of poetry and had indeed, when he stayed with Sir George Beaumont at Cole Orton, to listen to his host reading from *The Excursion* after dinner, there is no evidence that he had any particular admiration for the nature poetry of the Lake School. And yet their aims, translating the terms of one art into those of the other, were identical. Wordsworth declared his clearly enough; they were twofold: first, in his own words, "to make the incidents of common life interesting," "to chuse incidents and situations from common life and to relate and describe them, throughout, as far as possible, in a selection of language really used by men"; and, secondly, "to follow the fluxes and refluxes of the mind when agitated by the great and simple affections of our nature." These were his positive aims; negatively expressed, it meant getting rid of what he called "the inane and gaudy phraseology of the eighteenth century." Compare these aims with Constable's, as expressed in his prospectus to an album of engravings called *The English Landscape*, published in 1829:

"In art there are two modes by which men aim at distinction. In the one by a careful application to what others have accomplished, the artist imitates their works or selects and combines their various beauties; in the other, he seeks excellence at its primitive source, nature. In the first he forms a style upon the study of pictures, and produces either imitative or eclectic art; in the second, by a close observation of nature he discovers qualities existing in her which have never been portrayed before, and thus forms a style which is original. The results of the one mode, as they repeat that with which the eye is already familiar, are soon recognized and estimated, while the advances of the artist in a new path must necessarily be slow, for few are able to judge of that which deviates from the usual course, or are qualified to appreciate original studies."

We may compare that last sentence with Wordsworth's well-known statement about the necessity of each original poet creating the taste whereby he must be appreciated. And with Wordsworth's definitions of poetry we may compare Constable's saying that what is essential in painting is "a pure apprehension of natural fact," that "we see nothing truly until we understand it," that "the landscape painter must walk in the fields with an humble mind," which comes close to Wordsworth's prescription of "wise passiveness." These parallel aims should, if our method of criticism has any value, have their counterparts in the technique of each art, and, surely, a close analogy does exist between Wordsworth's practice in poetic diction and Constable's practice in painting. Wordsworth's return to the unaffected forms of speech, his rejection of the artificial diction which the seventeenth and eighteenth centuries had regarded as essential to poetry, is strictly parallel to Constable's rejection of the artificial mode of composition, the unnatural colouring and the rhetorical sentiment of the convention in painting during the same period. Both men pursued the same method, trying to realise in their art the fullest possible sense of the objectivity of the visible world. Doubtless they were driven to this method by their own individual needs, by their personal psychology. But we must also remember that this desire to affirm the actuality of the world of appearances is characteristic of the English mind, as represented by the empirical school of philosophy, and empiricism was very much in the air at the end of the eighteenth century. Constable may not have been very conscious of it, and we cannot, of course, impute to Constable's painting the philosophical significance of Wordsworth's poetry. But in making our comparison we are not thinking of Wordsworth's philosophy, but of his poetry, which is not necessarily the same thing. The comparison is between the painter's rendering of the actualities of colour and light, and those many isolated lines and images in which the poet brings to the mind of the reader the actual lustre and texture of natural objects.

The parallels are plentiful enough in this period—I think that perhaps an instructive one exists between Keats and Turner—Keats and Turner rather than Byron and Turner. But the comparisons now become more tenuous, perhaps because the arts are more eclectic, perhaps because it is in the nature of romanticism to confuse the categories, to make painters poetic and poets painterly. The extreme case is that of the painter-poet, represented, for example, by William Blake, and later by Rossetti. There are some people who decry Blake as a poet, others as a painter, but I feel fairly certain myself that his genius finds equal expression in both mediums. Whatever significance such a rare phenomenon has— and I shall deal with it at more length in the next essay—it does not affect our present enquiry. For the value which attaches to what I would venture to call the analogical method of criticism depends on keeping the manifestations of the separate arts distinct in separate individuals. In a case like Blake the geometrically impossible has happened: the parallels have met in some infinity of genius, and the conditions of our problem are thus cancelled.

What, finally, is to be learned from this analogical method? Perhaps only a reaffirmation of an old truth: that each art has its own laws of development, and reacts in its own way to the same conditions. But we can perhaps add this much in explanation of the divergent paths of poetry and painting. Poetry by its nature is anchored to a fixed point, the language of the country; and however much the social conditions change, the community must accept what the poets themselves dictate, or simply do without poetry. But painting, being independent of national modes of expression, is free and universal in its appeal, and it may well happen, and has happened disastrously in the history of English painting, that foible and fashion may turn against native art, and maintain for centuries a snobbish affectation for foreign modes. The history of our music is a still more melancholy witness to this truth. How far we resign ourselves to such a fact may in the end depend on our political convictions; for it is surely a significant fact that the eclipse of our native painting corresponds fairly exactly with the ascendancy of a wealthy oligarchy, able and anxious to cultivate tastes distinct from the common mass of people. Even if, as in Renaissance Italy, those tastes are satisfied at home, nevertheless they lead inevitably to dilettantism, archaicism, and every other form of artificiality. The development would be far otherwise in a community without distinctions of class and wealth, in which the artist plays a strictly functional part. Only some such ideal community would ensure conditions favourable to the parallel development of the arts in equal force and fullness.

ENGLISH ART

I

In any attempt to define the essential characteristics of English art (and that is to be the aim of this essay), we must begin with an explanation of what we mean by the word "English." Geographically we know what England is, and though there seems to be a good deal of doubt about the question, we could perhaps arrive at a satisfactory racial definition. But none of these senses would suit our purpose. Art has a way of defying boundaries, whether of land or of blood, and what we seek is actually a definition of something at once so subtle and so penetrating as the English spirit. Of certain works of art, say of the seventh and eighth centuries, we can say with confidence that they were made in England, and with the Celtic tradition to sponsor them, there is no reason to suppose that the artists were not natives of this country. But such works speak no English to us, and what we have to determine is at what period art does become specifically English, by style and not by provenance, and in what this English style consists. We can then attempt to trace this style in its various manifestations.

Matthew Arnold, in his *Study of Celtic Literature*, ventured to affirm that the Celtic races have shown a singular inaptitude for the plastic arts. To-day, with a considerably greater knowledge of the forms of their art, and of its psychological implications, no one would venture to be so dogmatic. The very contrast which Matthew Arnold draws between the German and the Celtic races, on a plus and minus scale, we would now rather regard as a direct opposition of modes of artistic experience. The basis of what Arnold regarded as the German superiority in this respect was "their fidelity to nature"—a basis which the Celts would instinctively have rejected. So when Arnold goes on to say that this inaptitude for the plastic arts "strikingly diminishes as soon as the German, not the Celtic element, predominates in the race," he is merely affirming his own particular conception of art. How that conception was still further limited is shown in the restriction he has yet to make on English art. "There is something," he says, "which seems to prevent our reaching real mastership in the plastic arts, as the more unmixed German races have reached it." He asks what European jury would give our greatest geniuses, Reynolds and Turner, the rank of masters along with Raphael and Correggio, Dürer and Rubens, and concludes that they lack in *architectonice*, a favourite word of his, by which he meant "the highest power of composition, by which painting accomplishes the very uttermost which it is given to painting to accomplish." Their success, such as it is, is of another kind; "they succeed in magic, in beauty, in grace, in expressing almost the inexpressible; here is the charm of Reynolds's children and Turner's seas; the impulse to express the inexpressible carries

Turner so far, that at last it carries him away, and even long before he is carried away, even in works that are justly extolled, one can see the stamp-mark, as the French say, of insanity. The excellence, therefore, the success, is on the side of spirit."

Though his argument is based on a limited conception of art, and more particularly on a misconception of classical art common to the eighteenth century (whose child Arnold was), nevertheless he has arrived at a conclusion which as a generalisation at first sight seems acceptable enough, and worth testing in a more detailed survey. Perhaps it does not amount to more than saying that English art has been predominantly romantic, and Matthew Arnold's further characterisation of our artists, as being "a little over-balanced by soul and feeling," and as "working too directly" for these, makes it quite clear that this interpretation of the matter was at the back of his mind.

That style which is the first to be distinct as a style, and to be associated with a racial blend that was henceforth to be distinctively English, was formed during the so-called Anglo-Saxon period—that is to say, during the two centuries which preceded the Conquest. About the origins of that style there are two opinions. English art historians, with a characteristic modesty, look abroad and find our inspiration in the Carolingian style. But other, chiefly German scholars, with what seems to me a finer critical insight, and a higher degree of historical probability, find the origin of this style in England itself—even assert that it was England which inspired the Carolingian schools. When it is agreed that this style has for its main characteristic a certain calligraphic or linear freedom, what seems more likely than the supposition that it was derived directly from the linear style *par excellence*, the Celtic style, which in these islands maintained its existence and its vitality long after it had disappeared from the Continent? This would seem to contradict Matthew Arnold's talk of Celtic inaptitude in the plastic arts, but I have already suggested that this was based on very incomplete knowledge.

This linear quality, "the bounding line and its infinite inflections and movements" as Blake was to express it, is clearly discernible in all types of Anglo-Saxon art—in the Alfred Jewel no less than in the Bayeux Tapestry, but most of all in the illuminated manuscripts of the Winchester school. Of the origin or foundation of that school we know nothing, and it is merely gratuitous to assume a derivation from the school of Rheims, which it most nearly resembles. The Winchester school and the typical contemporary Byzantine style of the Ottonian school stand apart not only in stylistic extremes, but also in extremes of geographic latitude, and it would seem natural to assume that what is intermediate not only in style but in position, namely the school of Rheims, was anything but a source of origination. But the point is of little importance; what is essential to recognise is the supreme vitality of the Winchester style, the most superb style in the whole range of medieval illumination. The earliest Winchester manuscript (the Charter of Edgar, Brit. Mus. Vesp. A. viii) is dated 966; the most famous is the Benedictional of St. Ethelwold belonging to the Duke of Devonshire, probably completed about 980. This latter manuscript represents the style in all its richness, and at the point of its greatest vigour. Here, indeed, is magic, beauty, and grace, and a capacity to express almost the inexpressible (or, as we might say, the divine); and as for *architectonice*, whatever that may prove to be when we come to analyse the claims of the classical style, we must conclude that it is something of no great importance if it is lacking here. The freshness and the freedom of these drawings, their incredible sureness, these qualities have often been noted and duly praised; but less than justice has been done to the high sense of form, the instinct for composition, displayed on every illuminated page. Two types of composition, one fixed and symmetrical, a rigid but crisp scaffolding, the other free and floating through the framework like a careless banner, play together in faultless harmony.

II

England, we might therefore say, in this tenth century stood for freedom and for grace; and these qualities were expressed as only they can be expressed in the plastic arts—by the infinite inflections of the line, the line which alone is capable of giving plastic expression to rhythm. Nothing proves the vitality of this style more impressively than its survival throughout the succeeding Romanesque period. Romanesque signifies static; in architecture, which is physically a static art, the new style triumphs naturally. The underlying linear rhythm is reduced to a fret round the massive arches. In sculpture, as notably at Malmesbury, the linear style survives unchecked; it is perfectly represented in the twelfth-century relief of the Virgin and Child in the Chapter-house at York. We find the style effectively translated into the new art of stained glass, reinforced here by the technical necessity of the lead lines. But illumination continues to be the distinctively English art, and though the Continental schools are now in full rivalry and the Winchester school has become a little outmoded, a little mannered (but can still produce a masterpiece like the Winchester Bible), there are now a number of English schools, all amazingly competent, and all decidedly English. They are English—the Bibles and Psalters from Bury St. Edmunds, St. Albans, Dover, Durham and York —in precisely the same characteristics, in their forceful linear rhythm, in their comparative freedom from Byzantine solemnity.

This brings us to a second general characteristic of English art which is perhaps present from the beginning—I mean what Ruskin, in rather shocked tones, called "our earthly instinct": "a delight in the forms of burlesque which are connected in some degree with the foulness of evil," a quality, Ruskin held, which has precluded our art from ever being properly sublime, and is present as a blemish in Chaucer and Shakespeare, and which renders "some of quite the greatest, wisest, and most moral of English writers now almost useless for our youth." But though he deplored this quality, Ruskin was honest enough to admit that "whenever Englishmen are wholly without this instinct, their genius is comparatively weak and restricted." At first sight it seems an odd quality to find, in combination with the spiritual virtues of magic, beauty and grace which we have already admitted; but if we do no more than rely on André Gide's observation, that in all great works of art extremes meet, we must be prepared to reconcile these two apparently contradictory qualities in English art. Actually, however, the contradiction only arises in minds bound, like Ruskin's and Matthew Arnold's, to a puritanical conception of spirituality, or to an idealistic conception of sublimity. It possibly did not occur to Chaucer or to Shakespeare, or to the earlier artists we are now considering, that anything created by God could be inapposite; and the whole virtue of the monkey in the margin, and of the grotesque in general, is that it should remind us of the immeasurable distance between the human and the divine.

Whatever the motive, it is certain that already in the eleventh century English art is characterised by a detailed observation of nature, a realism, by no means inconsistent with the absolute qualities of grace and rhythm conveyed by the linear conven-

ENGLISH ART

tions. The result is, that when the great change of
sentiment came over the Christian world in the
twelfth century, and a new movement of thought
began which was the prelude to realism in philosophy,
to humanism in science, to charity and simplicity in
religion (in short, Franciscanism) and to naturalism
in art, English artists were again ready to take the
lead. Indeed, no abrupt transition is observable in
English art. The line still dominates the composition.
It is suaver, more restrained in the interests of
realism, the sentiment expressed is sweeter. But it
is the same sentiment, in the illuminator of the
Benedictional of St. Aethelwold as in Matthew Paris,
and the same means are adopted to express it:
the linear style. How we regard the consequences
will depend on our æsthetic standards; if, with
Matthew Arnold, we regard "fidelity to nature" as
the only standard, then the English style, as we progress through the thirteenth and fourteenth centuries,
can only seem increasingly insular. And actually
that style itself could not hold out indefinitely against
the forces arrayed against it, chief of which was the
increasingly uniform character of Christian culture
in Europe. The Church was gathering its scattered
sheep into a closer fold, and in that closer fold the
communication of fashions became rapid and inevitable. It was not an age to encourage individuality
of any kind, and the English artist was to discover
that, in competition, his insular methods were ill-
adapted to express the exact shades demanded by
"fidelity to nature." The sentiments of humanism

are too vague to be bounded by a line. The line could still have its way—its erratic and unnatural way—in the depiction of the folds of a garment, and it had its way with a vengeance in such an English oddity as the Perpendicular style in architecture. It survives, in its persistent manner, well into the sixteenth century; but it is gradually petering out, and with it disappears an essential quality in English art, a quality which English art, in spite of the sporadic effort of William Blake, was to be long in recovering.

Not that the process of change was without its compensations. But unfortunately they do not belong to the plastic arts—they are to be sought in our literature, an art infinitely more resilient. There our other national characteristic, our earthly instinct, found full scope, and in the poetry of Chaucer and Shakespeare the most natural aspects of humanism found perfect expression; our spiritual quality being at the same time not inadequately represented by the *Faerie Queene*. By keeping a comparative view of the various arts one can realise the inadequacy of external causes, such as the Great Plague, to explain the disappearance of any one art. It might be suggested that the plastic arts, being so manual, are more dependent on an unbroken tradition; and that a catastrophe which left perhaps no more than one artist in ten alive to carry on such a tradition is a sufficient explanation of the different destinies. But that is to take a superficial and dilettante view of the craft of literature, which is no less dependent on its man-power and its accumulated wisdom. We are left to conclude that the plastic arts all but disappeared in England between the fourteenth and the eighteenth century simply because they were superseded by a more powerful and an alien mode. The quest which began with Giotto and Masaccio simply did not, and it might be said that for some reason it could not, enter into the plastic consciousness of an English artist. To enquire into the cause of that inability would take us too far from our present subject, and into the doubtful fields of social psychology. Whatever the cause, we have to confess that for four centuries an English art (which is different from art in England) did not exist.

If, as I believe, the source of our technical inspiration had failed in its depths, it might conceivably have happened that the other tributary to our national genius in art would have been strengthened. Our earthly instinct might have found a new mode of expression in the plastic arts comparable with the freedom it had found in poetry and drama. But here the essential distinction between the plastic and the literary arts becomes evident. Literature is a refinement, or at any rate a variety, of our normal and natural mode of communication. The plastic arts, on the other hand, are a special or abnormal mode, and depend on the perfection of an additional and, biologically speaking, unessential instrument. That instrument, in English art, had been the line. When the line, owing to the development of new instruments of plastic communication, no longer served its purpose, the whole equipment of the English artist was out-of-date, and he had no aptitude for the new instrument. He might, so long as he retained the line, have dispensed with medieval grace and spirituality, and then turned his earthly instinct to account. But in the circumstances he could only wait for a new plastic consciousness to evolve, and that takes centuries. Even in the native land of the alternative tactile values, a whole century elapses between Giotto and Masaccio. It would not have been too long to have waited two centuries in England. But meanwhile a very different consciousness evolved, a consciousness which not only inhibited any growth of the sensuous southern mode of spatial realisation, but which threatened and finally destroyed the earthly instinct in our literature: the moral consciousness of puritanism.

I cannot speak without prejudice on this subject, so I shall not dwell upon it. To anyone who is inclined to base his whole philosophy of life on æsthetic values, what we gained in moral fibre and eventually in economic prosperity by that change of spirit which culminated in the Reformation can never compensate for what we lost in magic, beauty, and grace. From any other point of view, social, religious, economic, a contrast has been drawn which is largely sentimental in its bias. But from the point of view we are concerned with, there is no possible confusion of values, because the contrast is between the presence and the absence of an indigenous will to art. Now and then, as in the miniatures of Nicholas

Hilliard, we may fancy we see a flicker of the national tradition. But actually it is not until the appearance of William Hogarth, and then only in its earthly aspect, that the English artist is once more conscious of his birthright.

III

Though Hogarth was openly and aggressively national in sentiment, the art of painting in England had for so long been dominated by foreigners that it would have needed a genius of the highest rank to restore the native tradition. With all his virtues, Hogarth was not such a genius; he was too dependent on the conventions of his age, and when he came to paint English scenes and interpret English life, the methods he employed were those of the Dutch and Venetian artists whose presence in the country he so much resented. But though he has his subtleties in the use of light and shade, and individuality in the disposition of his paint, his general attainments are not to be compared with those of a Tiepolo, a Vermeer, or even a Jan Steen. It is only in an isolated miracle like "The Shrimp Girl" that he gives us any indication of what he might have done had he thrown the foreign conventions to the wind, and so anticipated the nineteenth-century revolution. Nevertheless, Hogarth's is the first great name in what is known historically as the English school, and we should be doing violence to the facts if, for the sake of our categories, we refused to find anything

specifically English in his art. Baudelaire, in his
notes on certain foreign caricaturists, written in 1857,
deals with Hogarth and Cruikshank, and the specifically English qualities he finds in them are in effect
medieval qualities. "Je retrouve bien dans Hogarth
ce je ne sais quoi de sinistre, de violent et de résolu,
qui respire dans presque toutes les œuvres du pays
du spleen." What the French, and particularly
Baudelaire, imply by the Englishman's spleen has
never been quite clear to me. It is perhaps explained
by another sentence in Baudelaire's criticism of
Hogarth: "Le talent de Hogarth comporte en soi
quelque chose de froid, d'astringent, de funèbre.
Cela serre le cœur." Speaking on the same page of
another artist, Seymour-Haden, whom one is rather
astonished to find in such company, Baudelaire says:
"Dans Seymour, comme dans les autres Anglais,
violence et amour de l'excessif; manière simple,
archibrutale et directe, de poser le sujet." Though
the feeling, in Hogarth and Cruikshank, is of a
narrowly defined type, we are back again at Matthew
Arnold's stricture of the English artists, that they
are a little over-balanced by soul and feeling, and
work too directly for these. But what Arnold regards
as an æsthetic limitation, Baudelaire regards as a
positive virtue, the expression of an inevitable sentiment. But for Baudelaire, who had escaped from
the false identification of art and beauty, the
grotesque was a mode of the imagination, and moreover an intelligent mode ("l'intelligence du fantas-
tique"), and he is enthusiastic in his praise of Cruik-

shank's "abondance inépuisable dans le grotesque."
"Le grotesque coule incessamment et inévitablement
de la pointe de Cruikshank, comme les rimes riches
de la plume des poètes naturels. Le grotesque est
son habitude." And it is an English habitude, a
form of burlesque connected in some degree with
the foulness of evil, as Ruskin would have it; its
virtue being precisely in its realism, its refusal to
shut its eyes to the presence of evil in the world.

But the phrase, "the English School," does not
generally call to mind the names of Hogarth and
Cruikshank. The first, and in some ways the most
typical representative of this school is Thomas
Gainsborough. Here certainly there is no ambiguous
quality like spleen, but nevertheless there is something
so exclusively English about Gainsborough, that in
spite of all he owed to his predecessors in Italy and
the Netherlands, we should expect to find his
English character reflected intimately in his methods
of painting.

Reynolds, in his well-known tribute to Gainsborough, freely admitted him to comparison with
the great Italian masters, and yet held that his distinction as the founder of an English school rested
upon his originality. When artists communicate to
their country a share of their reputation, he said,
and so justify the appellation English, it is a portion
of fame not borrowed from others, but solely acquired
by their own labour and talents. But his analysis of
Gainsborough's originality is a little limited; he
mentions, "as the fundamental," the love which he

had to his art, and beyond that, his capacity for observation. "He had a habit of continually remarking to those who happened to be about him whatever peculiarity of countenance, whatever accidental combination of figure, or happy effects of light and shade, occurred in prospects, in the sky, in walking the streets, or in company. If, in his walks, he found a character that he liked, and whose attendance was to be obtained, he ordered him to his house: and from the fields he brought into his painting-room, stumps of trees, weeds, and animals of various kinds; and designed them, not from memory, but immediately from the objects. He even framed a kind of model of landscapes on his table; composed of broken stones, dried herbs, and pieces of looking-glass, which he magnified and improved into rocks, trees, and water." There is a naïvety about such a method which we English love, and Gainsborough was a naïve person. But we are far from an excess on the side of spirit; there is nothing here "a little over-balanced by soul and feeling, working too directly for these." And as we have already accepted Matthew Arnold's diagnosis of the national characteristics in our art, we can only conclude that by Gainsborough's time a profound modification had taken place. Reynolds's definition of his genius is of the familiar Carlylean kind—an infinite capacity for taking pains. It belongs to that aspect of English genius more typical of our science and philosophy—that gift for tireless detailed observation, the foundation of our reputation as empiricists. This gift was actually fostered by the Puritan tradition, with its general distrust of imagination and sensuous perception; and Hogarth, for example, was decidedly a Puritan moralist, a little overbalanced, shall we say, by virtue and indignation. But there was nothing of the moralist in the personal make-up of Gainsborough; his sensibility was pure of any prejudices external to its operations; which is to say that he was, like all great artists, predominantly a sensualist. Again, our earthly instinct. But in this case the instinct had a preceptor in Rubens, and a comparison of Gainsborough with Rubens might restrain our generalisations. Perhaps the racial differences involved are small—Gainsborough being a native of the least Celtic part of England, the part nearest to the land of Rubens. However much he gained from Rubens, however much Rubens is responsible for the change that came over Gainsborough in his Bath period, the differences between the two men remain wide. Gainsborough never sacrificed his spontaneity, his greatest gift, and he never, like poor Romney, attempted to emulate the grandiose conceptions of his foreign masters. He kept his feet firmly on English soil, and did not ever paint against the grain of his English temperament. And he is much nearer than any painter had been for three hundred years to the characteristic technique of our early artists. His thin brush strokes, deft and dexterous, feathery in their lightness—what do these express but a joy in linear rhythms, a desire for clarity and concision, for the determinate and the definite?

From a wider point of view, these are the classical virtues too—at least, the virtues of the classical technique. And the century of Gainsborough was to see a classical revival in Europe, not the first, and assuredly not the last. It is probable that none of the nostalgias for the past, particularly for the antique world of Greece and Rome, ever succeeds in recreating the reality of their life and art. Actually there was no unity in that world, and we are left to choose between the Greece of Parmenides and the Greece of Plato, or, as Nietzsche expressed it, between the cult of Dionysos and the cult of Apollo. Renaissance classicism seems to recover some at least of the superficial aspects of ancient life and ancient art, but the classicism of Reynolds and his French predecessors in the theory of art was surely based on a complete misunderstanding of the Greek point of view. A contemporary French critic, in a brilliant study of Nietzsche, summarises the distinction which Nietzsche laboured so passionately to make between a realistic and a romantic conception of classicism, and with some modification we shall find the distinction one that we can use to explain our dissatisfaction with eighteenth-century classicism. "Nietzsche," writes Monsieur Maulnier, "applied to classical art that critical gift which, more even than his gift as a poet or as a metaphysician, was his birthright. He first brought to light the fundamental virtue of such art—the perfect union of inner richness and tragic simplicity, of lucidity and violent instincts. The classical era is thus for him the apollonian era *par excellence*, that in which the passions only acquire their mortal profundity behind a rigid discipline, that of the *mask*. Classical man is masked; that is to say, Nietzsche finds in him, not only the strength of the most violent passions, but also the strength of an heroic hypocrisy, the art of self-mastery, the grand style. . . . When, analysing tragic realism, he observes that tragedy is metaphor, the transmutation of life into discourse, and is in consequence as far from pretending to imitate life as the musician is from imitating cries of passion in his music, he puts his finger on what is perhaps the central truth of classical art, and of great art in general, a mode of expression different from life, more perfect than life in that it avoids all clumsiness, insignificance and incoherence. No one, perhaps, has come so near to defining the enduring value of the classical discipline, which aims at rendering the most ardent and most audible passion, not at moderating or mutilating it. . . ." Now observe how subtly, but how vitally, this conception of classical art varies in Reynolds: "The whole beauty and grandeur of Art consists . . . in being able to get above all singular forms, local customs, particularities, and details of every kind. All the objects which are exhibited to our view by Nature, upon close examination will be found to have their blemishes and defects. The most beautiful forms have something about them like weakness, minuteness, or imperfection. But it is not every eye that perceives these blemishes. It must be an eye long used to the contemplation and comparison of these forms. The Painter who aims at the greatest style . . . corrects Nature by herself, her imperfect state by her more perfect. His eye being enabled to distinguish the accidental deficiencies, excrescences, and deformities of things, from their general figures, he makes out an abstract idea of their forms more perfect than any one original. . . . The idea of the perfect state of Nature, which the artist calls Ideal beauty, is the great leading principle by which works of genius are conducted."

It will be observed that Reynolds has left out the passions. His mask is perfect, his discipline rigid; but it is an abstraction, an intellectual calculation of the highest common denominator to be observed in the calm features of nature. What was meant as a discipline of the emotions, Reynolds converts into a discipline of the mind. The empirical bias of the Puritan, of the de-natured Englishman, triumphs in the last sanctuary of instinct and sensibility, and a stultification sets in. Well might Blake say that Reynolds was "hired by Satan to depress art."

Significantly, his art is the art of the portrait painter. His excursions into allegory and the heroic are not his happiest efforts. But in portraiture he could exercise his talent for observation, though he could hardly, by this means, arrive at an abstract idea of man. His gift was psychological; and beyond this, an infinite capacity for taking pains. Sometimes he so far forgets his principles as to achieve spontaneity, as in the portrait of Nelly O'Brien. Otherwise, and in general, he reflected the Englishmen about him; but this is too passive a role to have anything distinctively English about it. It is not the matter, but the manner, that is significant for this enquiry.

IV

The course of this argument leads inevitably to William Blake. For Blake embodied consciously and consistently the original characteristics of our art, and though the very universality of his genius involved technical limitations (for all the faculties and instincts have to be concentrated in one channel to ensure perfection of expression), he so clearly represents the national temper and with such power of imagination, that any judgment relative to these standards must give him the highest rank. The artists of the Middle Ages are anonymous; but of those who belong to subsequent ages, only Turner is of equal significance; and Turner, beside Blake, is intellectually naïve. Blake's reaction to Reynolds may be studied in his literary works. It is the reaction of a terribly sincere spirit to something he believes to be sham and sophisticated. Sure above all of the validity of his spiritual sensations, and of their superiority to all merely rational modes of apprehension, Blake set himself the task of making his vision determinate, of giving imagination an outline. His art is an attempt to combine the greatest intensity of subjective thought and feeling with the greatest clarity of objective representation. And that is precisely the character of all great art—of classical art in Nietzsche's right conception of it, of Christian art in its Byzantine and early Gothic manifestations, and of the isolated art of an individual like Blake.

Literally speaking, Blake was not completely isolated. His friend and contemporary, John Flaxman, is an artist who must be rehabilitated in the light of these considerations. His conception of classicism was superficial and rational; but it encouraged a linear technique, and the grace and delicacy of his line is in the English tradition. But it was not realised; it was not fed by a vision like Blake's. If only from his close association with Flaxman, Blake was conscious of the values of classical art, but he held that "we do not want either Greek or Latin Models if we are but just and true to our own Imaginations, those Worlds of Eternity in which we shall live for ever in Jesus our Lord." This is, of course, the voice of the mystic, but it is not easy to dissociate the mystic from the poet and the painter, and the genius is constant for every aspect of the man. That he did not use paint like a genius was a conscious choice rather than a personal limitation. He did not believe that the technique of oil paint was sufficiently definite for his purpose, and the failure of his experiments in tempera and other media was due to defective chemistry rather than to inefficient handling. When the chemistry is sound, as in his water-colour drawings, his illuminated printing and his "colour-printed drawings," the hand is sure and instinctive. And unless what Matthew Arnold calls *architectonice* is to be measured by the square yard, that quality too is present in the highest degree. Indeed, so powerful is the sense of composition in many of Blake's drawings, that they seem to transcend the scale and medium of their execution, and expand in our receptive minds to the dimensions of a Michelangelo or a Rubens. Nowhere else in the whole range of plastic art, unless in Giotto, is the capacity of the line for rendering three-dimensional form so amply demonstrated, and nowhere is solidity so compatible with movement and ethereal light.

That qualities more profound than style and technique are involved in the establishment of a tradition is shown by the fate of Blake's immediate followers—George Richmond, Edward Calvert and Samuel Palmer. Their engravings, woodcuts and watercolours have a lyrical appeal which is valid enough, but we feel that their inspiration is literary, and in the damning sense. Blake could take a poet's images and translate them into their visual equivalents, but his followers take poetic ideas and illustrate them. There is a world of difference—the difference between an equivalent and a derivative. It is a difference worth observing in certain contemporary movements.

The scope of this essay does not allow for the consideration of several artists of the eighteenth and nineteenth century who undoubtedly as individuals and as craftsmen occupy a distinguished place in the history of English art, but who are, in comparison with foreign artists, unjustly depreciated. Generally provincial in their origins, often self-taught and endowed with remarkable natural genius, they are too mute and inglorious to rise to a representative status. In a sense there is something very English about them all; their very eccentricity is English. They have English characters and they paint English scenes, but in the intimate or spiritual sense they are not English at all. Chief of these is Richard Wilson, who might as well have been a Dutchman or an Italian so far as he has any of our racial characteristics which find expression in his style of expression. And though superficially they reflect the forms and colours of our land and people, even such painters as George Morland and James Ward can be dismissed as in-significant for our purpose. The case of William Etty (and, a generation later, of Alfred Stevens) is almost pathological in its absolute denationalisation—its utter remoteness for any consciousness of an English tradition. But with the rise of the English school of landscape painting, which begins with Girtin and ends with Turner, we are once more face to face with a phenomenon which is completely and peculiarly English in its essence.

V

In its essence it would be possible to regard the English school of water-colour painting as a return to the grace, the clarity and the brilliance of our medieval illuminators. A pedantic designation insists on the term water-colour *drawing*, and the method is essentially a linear one. In a casual way, Ruskin somewhere draws a distinction between drawing with a brush and painting with a brush—a distinction which in our own time has been brilliantly elaborated by Heinrich Wölfflin. In Wölfflin's sense, the English water-colourists are always linear, and never *malerisch*. In its origins the method was used principally for topographical sketches, and it was chosen as a medium for this purpose precisely for its precision. That this technique was raised to the dignity of an art is due to the genius of Girtin, who in his short lifetime left sufficient masterpieces to determine the future course of English landscape painting. It is not often possible to prove an influence (which does not always imply an imitation), and in matters of technique a single revelation is sufficient to deflect the course of an artist's development. There is, of course, sufficient documentary evidence to show that both Constable and Turner studied Girtin to good effect; what must remain a matter of opinion is the extent to which the development of the later masters would have been retarded without the example of Girtin. Girtin, who died, we must remember, at the age of twenty-seven, was probably the greatest genius of the three; he impresses us by at once using his talents with intelligence. Not only his hand, but his mind was spontaneous.

It would be pushing our categories once again to

paradoxical limits to suggest that the English qualities of our water-colourists can be explained as a re-emergence of the basic linear signature of our race. There is much more to it than that. There is, in fact, a certain sublimity, product not only of line, but also of tone and composition and of the whole romantic conception of landscape, a conception not confined to painting, even finding its supreme expression in the poetry of Wordsworth. Mr. Laurence Binyon, in his interesting lectures on *Landscape in English Art and Poetry*, has suggested that this love of landscape was always present in our national character, being part of our Celtic heritage; he quotes an early Welsh poem by the bard Taliesin, and says "it is quite inconceivable that any poet of the classical tradition, any poet who had absorbed the Mediterranean mind, could have written thus, or indeed have written on such a subject. Taliesin identifies himself, as he sings, with the intangible, the invisible; with the wind that symbolises the mystery of the world." The validity of this comparison depends entirely on what Mr. Binyon means by the phrase "identifies himself . . . with the intangible, the invisible." In the fragment of the poem he quotes, the process is rather one of actualising the intangible, the invisible (in this case the wind); and though I am not familiar enough with Celtic poetry to express any opinion about its general character, I feel that the typically English attitude towards nature is always more objective than Mr. Binyon would imply. In my book on Wordsworth I have already pointed out how realistic, in his case, the so-called romantic attitude to nature was—how it was related to the empirical school of philosophy represented, in Wordsworth's time, by Hartley. Wordsworth's attitude towards nature is not, of course, a simple one—it is not what the psychologists would call a direct extrovert attitude. In his case it was a reaction from an opposite tendency. In his well-known note on his childhood he wrote: "I was often unable to think of external things as having external existence, and I communed with all that I saw as something not apart from, but inherent in, my own immaterial nature." This is certainly Mr. Binyon's state of identification. But Wordsworth goes on to say: "Many times while going to school I grasped at a wall or tree to recall myself from this abyss of idealism to the reality," and in my study of Wordsworth I suggested that his whole poetic development, in relation to nature or the outer world, was an attempt on the poet's part to recall himself from an abyss of idealism to the reality. That is how, I think, Wordsworth came to create the actuality and vividness of his visible world. It was a process of realisation, of objectification, determined by an intense psychological need. I suggest, therefore, that this Celtic strain in the English race, pressing us on, in Matthew Arnold's words, "to the impalpable, the ideal," is at once, as he would have it, the cause of our impotence in the higher branches of the plastic arts, but also, as he did not perceive, by a process of compensation or reaction perhaps induced by other elements in our racial blend, the cause of the minute particularity of our objective vision. Constable himself described his purpose as "a pure apprehension of natural fact." The phrase is perhaps more significant than he intended it to be; for "pure apprehension" implies something different from the analytical observation of the scientist, while "natural fact" warns us against any idealistic interpretation. Unfortunately we have no record of Constable's state of mind during childhood, but can we doubt, when the products are so similar, that it was of the same cast as Wordsworth's? Constable was humbler; it was not for him to "breathe in worlds to which the heaven of heavens is but a veil," not for him to pass Jehovah with his thunder and the choir of shouting angels, unalarmed. Compared with Wordsworth, as compared with Turner, he is without vision; but perhaps some deep common sense warned him of the instability of human visions. Certainly to-day, whilst we differ among ourselves irreconcilably about the genius of Turner, we accept the purer if more limited genius of Constable without reserve. We recognise that none of our artists has given fuller expression to our interest in natural phenomena, has more fully satisfied our desire to have these phenomena recorded in all their variety and aspects. But Constable does more than record; he communicates excitement by his method of recording—and does so, not merely by his deftness in seizing the actualities of light and colour and atmosphere, but by giving us a surplus which is the man himself, his sense of style and his creation of form.

VI

I have already said that there is no settled opinion
about the greatness of Turner. Some people, no
doubt, have been adversely affected by Ruskin's
eloquence, and by the completeness of his exposition;
for most critics are human enough to want to discover their own reasons for liking an artist, and it
may be doubted whether Ruskin has left unexpressed
a single possible reason for admiring Turner. But
when we have discounted personal prejudices of this
kind, we are left with obstinate questionings. A
comparison with Constable should quickly reveal
the differences involved. Turner studied nature as
humbly and intently as Constable. He was able by
his technical deftness to reproduce equally well and
perhaps with more ease the specific details of natural
fact. At a time when Constable was still fumbling
in the wake of the Dutch landscape painters, Turner
could produce such a magnificent transcript of
natural fact as we find in "Calais Pier"; and no
painting in the whole range of the naturalistic school
is so subtly and so truly observed as his "Frosty
Morning." But Turner was not satisfied to be fed
in a wise passiveness. He became inspired by what,
for want of a better phrase, I am in the habit of
calling a sense of glory. It is not quite fair of Ruskin
to say that "Constable perceives in a landscape that
the grass is wet, the meadows flat, and the boughs
shady; that is to say, about as much as, I suppose,

might in general be apprehended, between them, by
an intelligent fawn and a skylark. Turner perceives
at a glance the whole sum of visible truth open to
human intelligence." This is at once to depress
Constable's genius to a level below what is implied
in his expression "pure apprehension of natural fact,"
and to exalt Turner's genius to a universality which,
frankly, it did not possess. Rather than possessing
a universal mind, Turner was conscious of the qualities which such a mind gave to the art of painting.
He knew that such a mind, however much it grounds
itself on patient observation, must finally lift itself
on the wings of the imagination. Turner's emulation
of Claude, which has so often been treated as
technical in aim, is, as I conceive it, more imaginative. It was not Claude's light, nor his limpidity,
but his sublimity that Turner wished to rival. If it
were a question of technical achievement, Turner
must have been conscious that already in a score of
paintings, pictures like his "Windsor," "The Sun
rising through Vapour," and "Abingdon," he was
master of more effects than Claude, in his sedateness,
had ever attempted. And as Turner so triumphantly
demonstrated, there was no question of his hero's
superior sense of form. But in painting a subject like
"Dido building Carthage," Turner was trying to
demonstrate that with all his talents he too was
capable of this further grace, this apex of sublimity,
which justified the Grand Style. If Turner had been
satisfied with this achievement we should have the
measure of his limitations. He would have fallen into

the same error as Reynolds, and all his observation would have been dammed up against a static idealism. But largely through the medium of watercolour, Turner was gradually discovering what might be called the autonomy of colour. He was discovering that colours could be organised into a harmony independent of nature. So long as he confined himself to water-colours, the experiment could pass with its significance unobserved—however remote from nature, they could be regarded as studies that would be absorbed and corrected in some finished oil-painting. But with "Ulysses deriding Polyphemus" (1829) Turner boldly transferred his experiments to canvas, and the first stage in the revolution which was to lead to the modern position was completed (the second and final stage had to wait for Cézanne). Ruskin might ingeniously maintain that Turner's colours were after all natural colours, once you had abstracted the shadows from objects; but except in the sense that all colour is given in nature, his argument is a vain paralogism. From that moment, until he reaches the logical conclusion of his method in paintings like the "Interior at Petworth," Turner is on a path which leads him to what Matthew Arnold regarded as the verges of insanity, but which we, with surely a broader vision, regard as an alternative mode of expression to any conceived by Matthew Arnold. If we ask what, in the process and from Matthew Arnold's point of view, has been sacrificed, we are led back to the ambiguous phrase "fidelity to nature." Arnold would no doubt have murmured about his *architectonice*, but if by this he meant the formal organisation of the picture, we must claim that even in his freest harmonies, the order is adequate for the material. What has been lost is definition, and this is sacrificed for the sake of intensity. It is interesting to speculate on Blake's possible reaction to Turner's later work. It is natural to assume that he would have condemned it outright, as he condemned Rembrandt. But it is just possible that he would have hesitated, recognising that Turner, in destroying chiaroscuro, was on the side of the angels—without knowing it.

VII

By the strangest of destinies, all that was gained by Constable and Turner—all that was recovered of the native virtues of our art—was to be lost to France. The effect of Constable on Delacroix is one of the most dramatic events in the history of art, just as the letter written by a group of French Impressionists acknowledging their debt to Turner is one of the most moving.* I have no ready explanation for the seeming perversity of our national trend. It is hardly that the men were lacking. Stevens at least had all the necessary natural ability; so, I am inclined to think, had some of the Pre-Raphaelites, Millais and Madox Brown. But for some reason they shut

*Quoted by Clive Bell, *Landmarks in Nineteenth Century Painting* (1927), p. 136.

their minds against the modern consciousness revealed in the work of Constable and Turner, and escaped into odd sanctuaries of pedantry and snobbery. It is a phenomenon not confined to painting; in poetry the early Wordsworth is followed by the late Wordsworth, Keats by Tennyson, whilst, by contrast, in the freer atmosphere of France a Baudelaire emerges. It is, in fact, to something stultifying in the atmosphere of England that we must look for an explanation. And personally I cannot find it in anything else but that final triumph of the puritan spirit—our industrial prosperity. The true explanation of the Pre-Raphaelite movement is the Great Exhibition. Looking, as we may still do, through the pages of the sumptuously illustrated catalogue of the masterpieces of art and craftsmanship then displayed, we are revolted by the ugliness and vulgarity of every single object; but we cannot deny them, in the mass, an astonishing vitality. They are the expression of the taste of the age, and they are appalling and shameful; but granted the economic and moral ideals of the age, they are inevitable. Before such inevitability, the sensitive soul could only retreat.